H45 I5I 03

THE SECRETS OF HYPNOSIS: Tapping into your Subconscious

IVO VELLI

THE SECRETS OF HYPNOSIS

Ivo VELLI

Tapping into your Subconscious

BMT
MEDIA

BMT Media
Charter House 29A London Road, Croydon, CRO 2RE
www.bmtmedia.co.uk

Published in Great Britain in paperback by BMT Media in 2006

ISBN: 1-905717-04-0
ISBN (13) 978-1-905717-04-0

A catalogue record of this book is available from the British Library

TRANSLATED BY
Katerina Popova

EDITED BY
Mike Darton

COVER, JACKET AND INTERIOR DESIGN BY
Hristo Gochev

Contents

Introduction

Dear reader! Take a quick look at your library and you will see that almost all books need some kind of preface to introduce you to the essence of the work that you have decided to read. An introduction to a book dealing with a delicate subject – or, as in our case, a subject unfamiliar to the majority of people – is virtually indispensable. This bold claim – i.e. that we really know little if anything about hypnosis – is solidly reinforced by all the current (and, in most cases, false) myths about hypnosis.

- Hypnosis: a ritual shrouded in profound mystery
- Hypnosis: the magical gift of a select few
- Hypnosis: an echo of archaic mystical practices that has made itself heard in the present day.
- Hypnosis: a weapon of evil manipulative geniuses
- Hypnosis: a panacea, a "magic cure" tossed before the very eyes of all our "blind" modern healers
- Hypnosis: the best way to understand your loved one's secrets or to make your mother-in-law shut up
- Hypnosis: thief of free will and common sense

- Hypnosis: "All problems solved!"
- Hypnosis this, hypnosis that ...

Those who are aware how unfairly this phenomenon, which has accompanied us throughout human history, has been estimated, underestimated and overestimated, are still few and far between. And so are those who realise how hard it is to correct, even just slightly, the public mindset, in the face of all kinds of pseudo-scientific fare designed to satisfy the inevitable spiritual and cultural hunger. Hardly anyone would define the present situation as a particularly favourable one for changing the ideas and beliefs of any other reader who has for one reason or another picked up this book.

Actually, I am trying to imagine the kind of person that would start reading something on this sort of subject; I am trying to imagine *you*, dear reader.

Perhaps you are a scientist or professional in this field who is familiar with the serious studies on the essence and practice of hypnosis – in which case you here have an excellent opportunity to compare the main theories, techniques and details, and perhaps to add yet another point of view to your extensive knowledge of the subject.

Or you might have picked up this book because you have a concrete interest in using hypnosis for one purpose or another: you have decided to work towards self-improvement, therapy, research or experimentation, or simply to improve your communications skills. Unhappily, however, really useful literature on the subject is – to put it mildly – scarce. So now you can hopefully take yet another of the countless steps along the tortuous path to knowledge and thence to a sense of completion of purpose and satisfaction.

Or you might on the other hand have concluded that it is only esotericism and mysticism that provide the most satisfactory answer to the profound and pivotal questions which have been troubling you for ages, and that the very word "hypnosis" has riveted your attention and afforded you the hope of unlocking the secret door to hidden knowledge. In that case this is hardly the best book for you, because when someone is ready for knowledge it does not matter precisely how and in what form he or she attains it. And if you have already realised that there is no such thing as chance or accident in this mysterious yet perfectly ordered world, you might regard this book as yet another tiny piece of the jigsaw puzzle you are eager to complete. Because everyone must draw the benefits from every single thing by themselves. Because self-training is at the core of training. And because self-knowledge is at the core of knowledge.

I remember once when someone wanted to know if you could use hypnosis to make a person fall in love with you. The answer was: "You can do it without hypnosis too." It is hard (maybe impossible) to meet all the expectations and answer all the questions that might cross your mind, and – thank God! – the purpose of the book you are now holding is not to find answers but rather to prompt new, more appropriate, questions ... because we all know that properly formulated questions imply their own answers – it is just that not all answers can be verbalised adequately. At some point in our lives we have all tried to recount a dream in minute detail; to articulate our feelings, sensations, the truth or reality we have glimpsed; to describe how it feels to dream that you are flying like a bird or falling down a bottomless shaft in an instant that lasts for eternity, etc. In such cases we are inexplicably certain of the validity and power of our experience, but we also become aware of the deficiency of the language we normally use. We desperately try to explain to the other person, groping for words and phrases we have not used for ages. Sometimes we make up new words (just as children do) or we repeat one and the same thing over and over again in a different tone of voice, eager to stress that there is a difference. We gesticulate tirelessly in an effort to convey the full intensity of our sensations, and when we exhaust our entire verbal potential, we look with both hope and despair straight into the eyes of the other person, who smiles at us with sympathy, we nod vigorously and knowingly and, snapping our fingers, usually end with the words, "Well, you know what I mean…" Perhaps our only mistake in this is that we are trying to give someone else an explanation and an answer that is specifically an explanation and an answer for ourselves only – an answer that is clear and sufficient for *me* only, and that may not make any sense to anybody else. So, what this book offers are explanations and answers that are adequate for *me*. What I hope most of all is that they find a resonance in you in the form of new and appropriate questions that will point you in a useful direction – that will show you the unique way to your unique answers.

And before we proceed to the heart of the matter discussed in this book, I would like to draw your attention to something else – to an age-old and obvious truth, which is also expressly noted in one of the ancient sources of wisdom, the Holy Bible. No man can serve two masters

[Matthew 6:24] and remain equally loyal to both. Because I am in the difficult position of an author who is eager to avoid the pitfalls of an excess of customary self-confidence while sincerely trying to help raise the veil that shrouds the essence of hypnosis, I would paraphrase this statement as follows: a man can hardly be both frank and tactful. And it is on this point that everyone makes his or her choice. I believe that there are people who would condemn *my* choice, since if I were faced with such a dilemma I would not hesitate to reject the benefits of tact. For every dogmatic belief in a given theory, practice or – God forbid! – individual, is the surest way towards amputation of the spirit, towards amputation of the scientific, creative, public and individual spirit. So I will do everything within my power to keep the *spirit* of the modest book that you are now looking at pure and undistorted – because I know that there is no such thing as a small, medium or large piece of *spirit*. And if you think that what you read here sounds provocative and self-confident, you will find that you have two options – to chuck the book away in annoyance or to read on. Should you choose the first option, well, I thank you for the time and attention you have spared so far. If you choose the second, however, I must tell you that you have grasped perhaps the most important rule of our subject matter, which is: "If you want to succeed in hypnosis, you must above all truly and firmly believe in yourself." That is the most important thing, to begin with. Hesitancy and uncertainty are the surest way to failure.

So we can now move on with those who have found that it is much better to believe than to doubt unreservedly. A friend of mine used to tell me, "Look at me and try to learn more about yourself." This really helped me – so I can only say in the same vein: "Read the words in this book and try to find your own truth in them."

May this book help you find it, fellow-traveller!

Chapter 1
The History of Hypnosis

Archaic techniques of inducing the ecstatic state;
Hypnosis in the Middle Ages;
Pioneers of classical hypnosis; Hypnosis today

Perhaps I should start by giving some kind of definition of hypnosis so that we know what we are actually talking about. If the truth be told, however, I would have preferred to avoid a precise formulation of hypnosis, since no definition could cover the essence of the phenomenon in full. To define something is to limit it, to restrict it, to take away its freedom and confine it within the framework of concrete logical thinking. We thus entirely ignore its abstract essence, which can be grasped only by the abstract-creative aspect of our psyche. Yet either way, I cannot neglect the duty of giving an answer that is satisfactory at least for rational thinking about the topic in question. There are, of course, quite a few different views on this question, but we will deal with them later.

Before that I want to tell you a story that I believe is relevant to our present subject. There was a martial arts student who asked his teacher to show him exercises that developed speed. The teacher told him to increase his physical strength; to improve his flexibility; to develop his vision; to toughen the parts of his body with which he dealt blows; to master each blow to perfection and, then, the combinations of blows he had shown him; and so forth. The student objected:

"But all I asked for were physical exercises that specifically develop speed!"

Then the teacher told him:

"If your muscles are strong, they will move your body much more easily. If your tendons are flexible, they will restrict your movements to a far lesser extent. If you develop your peripheral vision, the information will reach your brain much faster. If your hands and feet are toughened, you won't hesitate to strike with all your power. If you master all the blows and combinations to perfection and are able to deal them even when you're woken suddenly, you won't waste time trying to remember them when you have to strike in real life.

"In addition, you must cope with the psychological barriers that prevent you from following your intuition. You must find your own particular way of improving your efficiency, because as long as you don't hear yourself but try to reflect on what others are telling you, you'll miss the right moment and lose valuable time for reacting, as you're doing right now."

And the teacher abruptly slapped the attentive student hard across the face.

"Speed is like a flower in bloom – all other qualities are simply the stem that leads up to it. The only way to attain speed is by developing every other quality you possess."

I am reminded of this story because, in exactly the same way, *hypnosis results from many conditions and factors that are in the same place at the same time.* Hypnosis is like a flower in bloom – the other conditions and factors are the stem that leads up to it.

Hypnosis is the subject of many books and in them is examined from various angles. Pioneers in the study of hypnosis tended to seek an answer to the question of the nature of the phenomenon in itself. Contemporary researchers into hypnosis concentrate primarily on the factors conducive to the induction of trance states. Let us take a quick overview of the history of the ideas advanced to elucidate this field of human knowledge.

Because there are plenty of accounts of the official history of hypnosis, however, this book means only to present a briefish sketch. If the subject is of special interest to a reader, he or she can find more detailed information in the References at the end of the book. Let us note at the very beginning that the somewhat immodest purpose of this otherwise modest book is not to repeat what is commonly known about hypnosis but to try to present in an accessible form the main principles of hypnotism and the applications of therapeutic trance.

Something else that should be noted is that this book is designed especially for a wide audience, since most of the expounded theories and practices are now textbook truths for professional scientists and hypnotists. We are all aware that where information is in favour of commercialism misinformation reigns supreme – in other words, it is not only that people today know very little about hypnosis, but also that what they *do* know is distorted by the commercial and irresponsible use of the term in the pseudo-scientific press and trashy health literature that has flooded the bookshops. It is a great pity that that is indeed the case, and I am well aware that this book is hardly capable by itself of bringing about the necessary positive change in people's minds. Yet I draw courage and faith from an ancient saying, according to which you can complete even the longest journey with the necessary number of steps – and I hope that this small book might be one of those steps. So let us focus on the first steps in the development of hypnosis.

The Viennese physician Franz Anton Mesmer (1734–1815) is officially regarded as the forerunner of modern hypnosis, and almost all historical accounts in this sphere start with him. The roots of hypnosis may, however, be traced back to the dawn of humanity, when shamans and priests performed healing as well as religious functions in the community. If we consult the serious anthropological studies of such scholars as Mircea Eliade, Claude Lévi-Strauss and Kenneth Meadows, we realise something else too – the trance as a phenomenon was not only familiar to the earliest civilisations but it was also a state consciously sought. The actual term *shaman* (or *šaman*) is thought to be of Tungusic origin and to literally mean "an excited or agitated person". Even a cursory examination of the subject points up the obvious analogy between hypnosis and archaic techniques of inducing the ecstatic state that were applied not only in healing but also in the instructing of new initiates.

With the advance of human society, the ancient rites, healing methods and magic practices were transformed into rituals that were acceptable to the newly emerging religious currents. If we examine the most popular religions and teachings – Christianity, Buddhism, Islam, Judaism – we at once again detect the presence of trance states. Every teaching simply seeks such states in its own way – you can enter a trance with the help of a lengthy fast, a vigil, through prayer, meditation, contemplation, in ritual dance, by breath control, by using hallucinogenic plants, etc. Even in the early Middle Ages various religious cults and orders used mass trances to effect cures, and some of those practices have survived in different churches and sects down to the present day.

In an effort to continue spreading its influence, the official Christian Church until the end of the eighteenth century mercilessly condemned and punished any arcane practice that was reminiscent of the ancient mystical cults. It was precisely at that time that the therapeutic trance was rehabilitated by Franz Anton Mesmer, the man who proposed the first structured theory of hypnosis accessible to a European way of thinking – the theory of "animal magnetism", according to which the hypnotist was capable of concentrating in himself a specific cosmic fluid. He was also capable of transmitting that same fluid to other people, thus inducing a therapeutic trance state. Mesmer's concept was not original even for his age, for his ideas were largely borrowed from Paracelsus and Richard Mead, a friend and follower of Isaac Newton. Mesmer's séances were, however, full of mysticism and they were extremely spectacular – especially his group cures, which inevitably involved the effect of psychic transmission, as is unavoidable in such a large group of people with similar symptoms and many things in common.

Nonetheless, irrespective of his ideological mistakes, Mesmer contributed to the development of certain psychotherapeutic techniques, and his popularity drew the attention of famous scientists and physicians to hypnosis, as a result of which one or two made some contribution to unveiling the mystery at the heart of the phenomenon.

One of the supporters of Mesmer's "animal magnetism" was the Marquis de Puysegur (1751–1825), who took a major step forward by associating hypnosis with sleep.

We should also give credit to an often neglected figure in the history of hypnosis – the Abbé José Custódio de Faria (1756–1819), who first studied the phenomenon from a psychological perspective in his only work, *De la cause du sommeil lucide*.

The term "hypnosis" – from Hypnos, the ancient Greek god who personified sleep – was introduced by the British surgeon James Braid (1795–1860) in his book *Neurypnology, or the Rationale of Nervous Sleep* (1843). Braid's concept was quite modern in that it gave special priority to the factors that influence the induction of hypnotic states. Braid emphasised the role of intense concentration on a single object or thought, and called this phenomenon *monoideism* – a term widely used by contemporary researchers of hypnosis and trance.

The theory of hypnosis also owes much to the late nineteenth-century French physician Jean Martin Charcot, who was the first to study hypnotisability (susceptibility to hypnotism) and to describe the three main levels or depths of hypnotic trance: light, medium and deep hypnosis. He defined those three stages – which are discussed in greater detail in the next chapter – respectively as lethargy (somnolence), catalepsy (hypotaxis) and somnambulism. According to Charcot, the deeper the hypnotic trance, the greater the submission with which the hypnotist's instructions are carried out. Charcot should also be given credit for developing interesting new techniques for hypnotic induction.

The ideas of another French physician and a contemporary of Charcot's – Hippolyte Bernheim – were very close to the modern concept of hypnosis. Bernheim put special emphasis on the role of *suggestion* and regarded hypnosis as a state of heightened, prolonged and artificially induced suggestibility.

In fact, many prominent scientists and physicians such as Freud, Pavlov, Binet, Janet and Coué applied hypnosis at various stages of their work.

A giant step forward in this field of knowledge was taken by the American psychologist Clark L. Hull (1884–1952), who pioneered experimental hypnosis and associated hypnosis with behaviourism. In a typically American manner, he disposed of everything that was superfluous and purged hypnotic practice of mystic ritualism. This important act laid the foundations of the modern scientific theory of trance states and phenomena.

And so by the mid-twentieth century hypnosis already had an appropriate place in world science and medicine, and its ever wider use was accompanied by major progress in research.

We must note that the main dispute concerning hypnosis in the academic community today is whether hypnosis is really an altered state of consciousness or simply unconscious role-playing according to Theodore Sarbin's theory. The proponents of both views have serious grounds on which to uphold their respective positions. My entirely personal opinion is that hypnosis is *an altered state of consciousness*, since people in a hypnotic trance have access to physical and mental phenomena that are otherwise inaccessible to them. It would be all too easy to assume that the truth is somewhere in between, but that position would hardly be helpful in any way. Dealing with the most indefinite aspect of human nature – the unconscious – in the constantly changing conditions of the unique trance state is an extremely delicate pursuit, and cannot be based on guesswork or personal preferences. For this reason, if we still lack irrefutable proof of the truth of either of the two views mentioned above, we are simply obliged to accept one of them – because the choice of approach and technique in our practical work depends on our choice of theoretical frames of reference. This book is not in any way intended to defend any particular theory, however. What we may actually take the liberty of doing is share our opinion on the question, as well as our arguments.

Fortunately, the dispute over whether hypnosis is or is not an altered state of consciousness concerns theory only, and certainly does not prevent the ever wider use of hypnosis. In fact, if we think about it, we will see that any practice that yields positive results can be cloaked in an adequate and logical theory, but not every well-sounding theory can pass the test of practical verification.

If we think about it even more carefully, we will recall that the consciousness of all of humanity and human history has been repeatedly altered dramatically by discoveries that have exploded the hitherto dominant theories. The catalysts of progress have been intellectual revolutionaries such as Copernicus, Galileo, Lobachevsky, Einstein and countless others. Such a revolutionary in the field of hypnosis is Milton H. Erickson (1901–1980), whose presence and ideas divided hypnosis in the mid-1970s into traditional and Ericksonian (non-traditional). In this case, however, the concept of tradition seems somewhat strange, considering that the principles of Ericksonian hypnosis have an analogy in practices that existed centuries before Mesmer and his popular recognition as the inventor of a new method of influence and therapy. What Erickson's ideas and those ancient practices have in common is the conviction that *hypnotic trance is a natural condition of the human psyche that is intrinsic to every person if the respective conditions and factors are in place*. It is not accidental that the latest trend in hypnosis – neuro-linguistic programming or NLP – has borrowed its ideas precisely from Erickson and his "non-traditional" approaches – which only goes to show that every new topic is actually an old topic temporarily forgotten. Yet let us first say a few words about Milton H. Erickson.

Erickson is undoubtedly one of the most colourful and charismatic figures in the history of psychotherapy. Erickson's influence on the development of hypnosis was due not only to his scientific notions and extremely interesting and effective techniques but also to the unusual trials and tribulations that fate had in store for him.

At the age of 17 Erickson was completely paralysed by an acute form of polio. All but he himself were resigned to his inevitable demise. Yet by an almost superhuman effort of willpower he regained control of his limbs, and those were his first steps along the path to personal success and a full life. Although his health remained frail throughout his life (he had a bad limp; he was colour-blind and saw everything in shades of purple; his hearing was poor; only half his diaphragm worked; he had almost permanent migraine; his mouth was partly paralysed; and he spent his last years in a wheelchair), Milton H. Erickson is remembered by the people lucky enough to know him as an extremely happy and strong person with tremendous vitality and an insatiable, childlike curiosity. At the same time, he was an ordinary down-to-earth person who took pride mainly in his stable marriage and eight children.

What is important for us, however, are Erickson's principles and methods, which ushered in a new era in hypnosis and psychotherapy. We will examine those principles in detail later on. At this point we will note only that it was on the basis of them that John Grinder and Richard Bandler – both students of Erickson – invented NLP (neuro-linguistic programming), the latest and increasingly popular trend in hypnotherapy. And since we have come to things that belong to the present day, perhaps it is time to stop talking about the history of hypnosis. Let us move on to hypnosis itself.

Chapter 2
Trance

The essence of trance and trance experiences;
Levels of hypnotic trance;
Trance phenomena; Trance indicators

If we had to define hypnosis in a couple of words, we could safely say that hypnosis is a *state of controlled trance*. It is for this reason that we cannot discuss hypnosis without discussing trance.

Trance is a mental phenomenon that is experienced by every person. To enter a state of trance means to transcend the boundaries of normal perception; to break free from what we call "incontestable reality"; to invalidate the laws that define and maintain the integrity of the familiar world; and to have direct access to phenomena that are inaccessible to the "normal" state of consciousness. The farther you go in the course of this "transcendence", the deeper the trance.

The supreme art of the shaman was to immerse himself in a trance while retaining control over his trance state – in itself, an act of magic. In the modern aspect of hypnosis things are considerably more acceptable, since the roles are divided – the hypnotised individual takes the role of falling into a trance, and the hypnotist that of controlling and ensuring the normal experience of this trance.

In fact, we have all had first-hand experience of trance states, in most cases without being aware of it. Proceeding from neurophysiological studies, one of the leading contemporary practitioners and researchers in this field, Ernest Rossi, devised the *ultradian theory* of human chrono-biological rhythms, according to which every person falls into a state of natural susceptibility to trance every 90 minutes or so. These are the so-called common everyday trance states which last from several seconds to several minutes.

We all know what it is, for example, to be doing a household chore and to become so engrossed in our work that we have no idea precisely when and how we cut or bruised our finger. At that instant we have spontaneous anaesthesia – which is a trance phenomenon.

We also know what it is to forget someone's name seconds after learning it – this is spontaneous amnesia, another trance phenomenon.

Or we might look for our keys or something else on the table until we suddenly realise that they have been lying right there before us, only we did not see them until then – this is spontaneous visual negative hallucination: yet another trance phenomenon.

In sum, there are countless examples and we all find

ourselves in one or several such situations every day. And that is because trance is an integral part of our psychic functioning.

Now let us consider in greater detail how the human psyche works.

We all know that our brain is made up of two symmetrical hemispheres – left and right. Those two hemispheres handle the transmitted information in a different way, and they also control different parts of our physical body. The right hemisphere controls the left part of our body, and vice versa. Most often, one of the two hemispheres dominates the other. Also, the two hemispheres normally have opposite functions. The left one accounts for verbal processes, whereas the right one operates with images. The left hemisphere thinks in linear and concrete terms, and the right in multidimensional and abstract terms. The left hemisphere is logical, intellectual and analytical. The right hemisphere is emotional, intuitive and holistic.

If the brain is a physical, material organ that can be seen and touched, the psyche – the invisible and immeasurable part of us that "moves" everything – is certainly not. It is much harder to study the human psyche. But what we do know for certain is that similarly to the brain, the psyche consists of two main parts, which likewise have different functions. Those two parts are conventionally called *conscious* and *subconscious*. We could also call them the *conscious* and the *unconscious* part of our psyche. A parallel is drawn between the characteristics and functions of those two parts in *Table 1*.

Table 1

CONSCIOUS	SUBCONSCIOUS
• Sometimes passive – e.g. when asleep.	• Always active from birth.
• Acts in an organised way.	• Follows instincts.
• Seeks logical solutions	• Prefers emotions.
• Operates with concepts.	• Operates with images and metaphors.
• Interprets information received.	• Takes everything literally.
• Critiques, judges.	• Takes things uncritically.
• Easily handles negative constructs.	• Does not identify negative constructs.
• Perceives time and space linearly.	• Perceives everything as occurring here and now.
• Avoids inner silence.	• Prefers inner silence.
• Maintains an illusion of control.	• Is stronger, but stays in the background.
• Needs effort and will to perform its functions.	• Has natural healing mechanisms and performs its functions spontaneously.

Naturally, this short table does not show all the characteristics and functions of the conscious and unconscious parts of our psyche, but the important thing to remember is that when we are in a trance our subconscious prevails. That is also why when we succeed in somehow eliminating the dominant role of someone's conscious mind and this gives us access to the unconscious part of his or her psyche, we can say that we have put him or her in a trance. If we also know how to control this trance, we can say that he or she is under hypnosis.

As phenomena, trance and hypnosis have always been the subject of one or other form of principled debate. That is because there is no exact way of measuring a given phenomenon. Nevertheless, we need some kind of theoretical basis and standard that would help us in practice. In Chapter 1 we mentioned Charcot's classification of the levels of hypnotic trance, which has essentially remained unchanged down to the present day. We said that there are generally assumed to be three main levels of hypnotic trance. The first and most superficial level – *light trance* (often known as somnolence) – is characterised by a distinct sense of physical relaxation, and a disinclination to move or speak. Quite commonly, subjects do not perceive this as hypnosis. They describe afterwards how relaxed and refreshed they felt; how they could have done or said anything they wanted, but they didn't do so because they didn't want to interrupt this pleasant relaxation and comfort. When people are in a light hypnotic trance, they can easily recall everything that happened during the session: they have a sense of time and can take the initiative (for example, they can easily end the trance if they want to).

Medium trance or hypotaxis is a deeper level of hypnosis in which people are much more open to their memories and emotions and have considerably less conscious control. Suffice it to say that *partial* manifestation of all phenomena typical of a trance, as described below, is possible at this level. An example of such partial manifestation might, say, centre on age regression. If it has been suggested to the subject that they go back to the time when they were five years old, after or during the session they will explain that they saw themselves at the age of five – unlike the experience that they would have if the same suggestion was made under deep hypnosis. Under deep hypnosis, they would say that they *are* five years old.

In fact, what is potentially useful to us are primarily the phenomena to which we have access in a deliberately induced trance. *Deep hypnosis* or somnambulism is the state that displays most, if not all, trance phenomena. However, we should not make the mistake of assuming that the level of hypnotic trance is stable and constant. On the contrary! The trance state changes constantly in the course of a hypnotic session, moving from light to deep in less than a minute, and vice versa. This should be kept in mind because the hypnotist must communicate with the hypnotised individual in a way that is specific to the respective trance level. The hypnotist must know at every single moment to which phenomena he or she has access and be able to adjust his or her instructions accordingly, for the surest way of impairing communication with a subject is by asking him or her to do something unfeasible. That is when we lose rapport, trust and, to a large extent, any chance of fulfilling the task we have set out to achieve.

Now let us list the most important characteristics of a trance.

Monoideism is the main characteristic of trance states. As the term itself shows, this means that the hypnotised subject's attention is concentrated on a single idea, image or object. Whenever our consciousness is active, our mind weaves an endless chain of separate thoughts and notions which constantly generate themselves – each thought generates a new one, which it supports or challenges, and then expounds or elaborates. If, for instance, the notion of "cup" pops up in our mind, it will immediately be followed by other notions and things we have learned in various ways about cups – what they are used for, what they are made of, who broke one of our favourite cups at our last party, who we really think of as a friend, and whether they reciprocate, etc.

We are in a constant state of inner self-dialogue. On the basis of our experience, for example, we say what is feasible and what isn't; what's right and what's wrong – and yet we go on asking ourselves if our beliefs are right. In a state of sleep or trance this inner dialogue is interrupted because of the absence of the conscious mind which keeps it up, and in such a state our entire mental potential can concentrate on a single idea or object. This is an incredible achievement of our perception, since this is the only case in which we perceive things as they are rather than as they are presented to us by the smaller part of our psyche – our conscious mind, moulded by our environment.

We should also note that trance is characterised by *full concentration of attention on inner experiences*. The hypnotised subject's attention may also be focused on external stimuli (light, a crystal ball, a particular tune or sound, the hypnotist's words, etc.), To induce a really deep trance, however, we must direct those projections inwards in a way that turns them into something intimate and personal for the subject.

Another characteristic of trance is *ideodynamics*. This means that things – whether suggested or not – for people in a trance seem to happen of themselves, without the individual's active physical interference. The idea of something is enough for the thing in question to manifest itself. What the hypnotist actually does is to suggest ideas that are then validated in the trance state appropriate for the purpose.

Trance is also distinguished by extremely *flexible perception of the spatio-temporal modality*, which makes possible such trance phenomena as age regression and progression. People under hypnosis usually lose the ordinary sense of time. For them hours might flash by in a second, and vice versa. Space may also be perceived in a new way – absolutely complexly, involving all our senses in full. The ease with which our subconscious mind plays with some of the most incontestable (at least until Einstein) parameters validating our reality is truly amazing.

Trance states also involve a *change in sensory perceptions*. This change may be full or partial – only the auditory, visual or kinaesthetic perception may change. The respective trance phenomena are hypnotic hallucinations of all kinds.

Also typical of hypnotic trance is *motor-verbal retardation*. People in a trance usually find it difficult to speak or move, unless the hypnotist suggests otherwise.

An interesting phenomenon is *trance logic*, which differs from logic in the normal waking state. In trance logic, two mutually exclusive propositions may co-exist without any conflict – i.e. a person may be both here and there, both now and then, and will regard this as normal.

Trance is also characterised by the *metaphoric processing of information*. This is particularly important for the therapeutic use of trance, because by means of the processing of information in the form of symbols the hypnotised subject understands and perceives everything that happens in correlation with himself or herself.

We should note at this point that in each of us the conscious mind has been taught to use signs in receiving, processing and transmitting information, whereas the original part of the psyche – the subconscious – operates with symbols. The difference between signs and symbols is of paramount importance, because signs present information in a linear temporal sequence whereas symbols can say everything simultaneously. It is much harder to read symbols than signs. To read symbols you must largely break with standard linear logical thinking. Yet in most cases this proves much harder than learning to apply standard linear logic.

To get an even better idea of the difference between signs and symbols, we could compare our alphabet with the ideogrammatic script of the Japanese.

When we want to convey some information in writing, we have been taught to use letters which we arrange in a line one after the other, thus creating words which we also arrange in a definite linear grammatical order for the purpose of forming a sentence that best expresses our particular thought.

To fulfil the same task the Japanese might well use a single ideogram, which contains all necessary parts of speech – verb, noun, adjective, etc. – and include many more temporal and spatial connotations.

In the first case our eyes pass over all sequential signs and words in the sentence before we start associating the information with definite thoughts and feelings, whereas in the second we perceive everything at once, and simultaneously with the emergence of thoughts and feelings we continue studying the other nuances of the concrete symbol.

Either way, we can say that the conscious mind necessarily needs logical clarity in order to perceive something, whereas the subconscious does not require such clarity – it does not reject anything and perceives everything.

The position of the conscious mind is that if there is a "yes" there cannot be a "no", and vice versa.

The position of the subconscious is that there can be both a "yes" and a "no" as well as something else, both at the same time and all together.

That is precisely why Milton Erickson says that *the sense of freedom is inherent to trance.* And that is also precisely why we need trance: to touch this freedom and the possibilities of which we only have a vague awareness – an awareness that reminds us of our spiritual essence and inspires our quest for constant self-improvement; an awareness that tells us that it might be more important to buy a particular book than to buy bread; an awareness without which we would not differ from animals.

Before we move on, let us repeat the most important phenomena – in other words, our untapped physical and mental potential – to which we have access in a trance.

Age regression is the ability to perceive time in a different way. With the help of age regression we can restore every single moment of our life with absolute precision, because we never forget anything – we are simply not always capable of reproducing it in what is assumed to be the normal state of consciousness. Age regression helps activate not only the mental but also the physical memory of the body. For example, if we suggest to a person under hypnosis that he or she is in third grade and ask him or her to write something, he or she will do so in the handwriting he or she had as a third-grader. Because unlike for us, the experience for him or her is real and actual.

Mentioning regression in time inevitably raises the question of a return to past lives and of reincarnations.

This question is examined in detail in Chapter 8, and we therefore do not deal with it here.

Some researchers of hypnosis also talk of age progression, in which the hypnotised individual can transport himself or herself into the future. I certainly do not want to deny any human ability that has been insufficiently studied, but in this case it must be expressly noted that we have, rather, a heightened ability to plan or predict things that are important for us as individuals. We know that prediction is a matter of available information. The point is that in most cases we are not aware how much information we really have on a given question. So when under hypnosis we have access to our information "storehouse" – the subconscious – we have a much better chance of accurately predicting the possible development of the things that are important to us. Otherwise – i.e. if we assume that people are indeed capable of transporting themselves into the future – the main job of hypnotists would surely be to obtain the winning numbers in the coming week's lottery.

Another trance phenomenon is our ability to manipulate our perception. This results in all kinds of hypnotic hallucinations. Hallucinations are mental constructs, even if they might have been produced with the help of sight, hearing, touch, smell or taste. Hallucinations can be positive – i.e. when we perceive something that is non-existent for other people – and negative, when we do not perceive something that is perceived by everybody else. *Hypnotic dissociation* is also a kind of hallucination – e.g. when someone can feel his or her arm separated (dissociated) from the rest of the body or when subjects perceive themselves in two or more places at the same time.

We have all heard that it is possible to operate surgically on a hypnotised person without anaesthesia and that he or she would not feel any pain whatsoever. Such anaesthesia is another hypnotic phenomenon, which, however, could safely be defined as a kind of tactile hallucination, because the opposite is also possible – we can cause an actually non-existent pain.

Amnesia and *hypermnesia* are also very interesting trance phenomena, which usually appear spontaneously in deep trance as further proof of the unusual potential that lies dormant within us.

We must also note the fact that a subject's entire physical potential can be mobilised and activated under hypnosis. It is a scientific fact that if a person simultaneously contracts all the muscle fibres in the body, he or she is capable of lifting a 25-tonne weight. With the appropriate suggestions, each one of us can be made to perform incredible physical feats. Perhaps it should also be noted here that when a person is in a hypnotic trance it is possible to control the functions of his or her autonomic nervous system – we can cause sweating, trembling, a change in the heartbeat rate, the slowing or total cessation of the blood flow, etc.

Actually, the use of the above-mentioned trance phenomena for therapeutic purposes constitutes hypnotherapy, which may be of help when combined with almost all other forms of therapy – general medicine, surgery, psychotherapy, dentistry, etc. Certain specific trance phenomena can be especially useful, depending on the specific purpose of the therapy involved.

In respect of dentistry, for example, especially useful for dentists are hypnotically induced phenomena such as anaesthesia, the reduction of salivation and blood flow control – particularly in the cases of patients who are allergic to certain medicines. Perhaps it should be noted here that suggestive and hypnotic influence offers dentists an excellent opportunity to cope with the commonplace yet widely ignored problem known simply as "fear of dentists" or dentophobia.

On the other hand, trance phenomena such as time regression and progression, amnesia, hypermnesia and hypnotic hallucinations play an indescribably important role in almost all aspects of psychotherapy.

To be able to make use of the trance state, then, we should be able to identify trance states in other people (since we hardly ever think of looking for them in ourselves). It is therefore essential to know what are the main indicators that show that a person is in a state of trance.

- The eyes usually give us the greatest amount of information about the state of the other person. What we usually see in someone in a trance is a fixed gaze, reduced blinking and drooping eyelids.
- We almost always detect reduced physical activity and muscle tone.
- We also note a difficulty in vocalisation or a disinclination to speak at all.
- In addition, we perceive a definite change in breathing. Breathing usually becomes slower, deeper and more even, but it could also be fast and uneven if the hypnotised individual undergoes some intense inner experience.
- Another trance indicator is the absence of facial expression.

- Another important indicator is an absent or weakened response to the surroundings – e.g. the subject will not react to a noise in the room or to an unusual action or behaviour on the part of other people.
- Facial colour usually changes too – this change might be obvious or barely discernible.
- If we make a person in a trance speak, we note a change in the voice – it usually becomes quiet, almost a whisper, monotonous, with a different intonation.
- Very often there are spontaneous ideomotor movements.
- We are able get a fairly good idea of trance depth from the hypnotised subject's speech, which becomes literal and unambiguous.

The best way to memorise those indicators is to practise and to develop a habit of identifying them. If you want to master trance and hypnotic techniques, try the following simple exercise.

Because every person naturally enters a brief state of trance several times a day, you could use your time on the bus or in a café to observe the people around you. In the appropriate situation you could try to identify indicators that someone is actually in a trance state – reduced muscle tone, slow breathing, relaxed facial expression, catalepsy, ideomotor movements, etc.

And if at some point during the exercise you try to look at yourself too, you may realise that you too are in a trance, since concentration of attention is, as noted above, one of the main trance characteristics.

Most interesting of all will be the question you might well ask yourself at this particular moment: *Am I really in a trance, or is this simply autosuggestion inspired by what I read in that book some time ago?*

Then some may well go on to ask themselves: *And would this question ever have occurred to me if I hadn't read it?*

Perhaps some readers are also wondering at this very moment why I should have included such potentially confusing questions. Let me tell you why. Because I need to make it easier to explain things in the next chapter, which deals with suggestion in hypnosis.

Chapter 3
Suggestion in Hypnosis

*What is suggestion?; Suggestion in the waking
state, under hypnosis
and posthypnotic suggestions; Suggestibility and
hypnotisability; Suggestibility tests*

According to a popular definition, hypnosis is sleep induced by suggestion. In principle, in this sense, *to "suggest" something to someone is to make him or her believe in it unreservedly by means of words or actions.* If by means of words or actions we succeed in making people believe that they will fall asleep or into a trance and yet be able to hear our voice and carry out our instructions (I am deliberately avoiding the word "commands"), we will have induced a hypnotic or suggested trance in them.

A rather outdated concept would define hypnosis as verbal or nonverbal influence on someone's thoughts and actions irrespective of – or even against – their will. Let us expressly note that hypnosis is actually a specific type of interaction, and *not* counteraction.

Hypnotism is a process that aims to align the mood, thoughts, actions and purposes of the hypnotist and the hypnotised subject, thus achieving rapport. The role of the subject is as active as that of the hypnotist – the tasks of the subject simply differ from those of the hypnotist. Let us repeat that the task of the subject is to experience a trance, whereas the task of the hypnotist is to ensure the proper occurrence and use of this trance.

Things change if we perceive this process as one involving domination – i.e. how one person should take control of another's will. In that case we could hardly talk of rapport.

In fact, our task is to make the person whom we want to influence yield control over his or her will voluntarily and, at that, enjoy it. Perhaps some might think that this is a contradiction in terms, but they would be wrong. And it is precisely here that the subtleties of the specific hypnotic communication (discussed in detail in Chapter 6) lie.

What we should always keep in mind is that people find it easiest to believe what they *want* to believe. That is also why it is easiest to suggest to someone something that they want to be true.

Otherwise, suggestion is all around us. We are almost permanently in the position of people who give or respond to suggestions – whether consciously or unconsciously. That is why there is no need to try to persuade anyone of the role of suggestion in our everyday life. The power of suggestion is most commonly displayed in the mass media – from commercials to political campaigns. And if we explore this subject further, we find that it is much easier to make people vote for a particular politician or party than to make them buy a particular brand of cigarettes or washing powder. So as to avoid being tainted by politics, I will finish what I mean to say on this matter merely by noting that public consciousness is extremely easy to manipulate. We should therefore pin our hopes for original and unbiased thinking solely on the individual consciousness of people who can resist the attacks of commercialisation and vulgarity in all spheres.

Talking of suggestion in hypnosis, we must mention the French physician Émile Coué (1857–1926), one of the most active and productive researchers of the role of suggestion and autosuggestion in therapy. He is also known for encouraging his patients to say to themselves 20 to 30 times each night before going to sleep, "Every day in every way, I am getting better and better." He also discovered that delivering positive suggestions when prescribing medication proved to be a more effective cure than prescribing medication alone.

Yet the main reason for mentioning Coué in this chapter is his *Laws of Suggestion*, the recognition and observance of which bring us closer to a correct concept of hypnosis and, consequently, determine the effectiveness of our work.

Coué's first law is the *Law of concentrated attention*: when attention concentrates on a single idea over and over again, it spontaneously creates a tendency towards implementing the idea.

The second law is the *Law of reverse effort*: the harder a person tries to do something, the smaller are his or her chances of success.

Extremely important for us is the *Law of dominant affect*, which states succinctly: the stronger affect replaces the weaker one.

It is easy to see that the above-mentioned postulates are distinguished by brilliant simplicity – and perhaps that is why they have been overlooked by many therapists who complain of the inefficiency of the available arsenal of techniques and concepts. In their case, however, maybe a lack of self-confidence, combined with a fear of discovering the truth, is stronger than any healthy aspirations towards knowledge, and Coué's third law applies with full force.

Now let us consider in greater detail the role of suggestion in hypnosis and try to classify suggestions by some criteria.

Suggestions may, then, be *verbal or nonverbal* and *direct or indirect*. This division, however, is conventional only – for the convenience of scientific research and instruction – because in everyday life it is impossible to differentiate between, for example, verbal and nonverbal expression. Imagine that a young man tells a girl that he is in love with her, comparing her eyes to crystal-clear lakes, her lips to a fresh rose, and her face to a wonderful mirage that constantly hovers before his eyes while, at the same time, his voice is entirely flat, his face remains impassive and his eyes are glued to a sports paper. Well, in such a case I fear that the boy must rely not only on the blindness but also on the deafness of love, as well as on the absence of logic in love. And to avoid banalities of the *love-is-a-sort-of-hypnosis* kind, we will return to our subject seriously and note that synchrony between verbal and nonverbal expression is a major factor that determines the power and effect of our suggestions. The explanation is simple – when there is such synchrony, the other person receives a single message only, whereas in the second case he or she must choose between the meaning of our words and the conflicting information we have transmitted in the form of nonverbal signals. Yet when the conscious mind is faced with such a choice, its critical faculty is turned on full force – which is precisely what we want to avoid when trying to induce trance.

We must say that the division of suggestive influence into direct and indirect is just as conventional. This is simply because we are not capable of recognising and controlling every single aspect of our behaviour.

Thus, direct suggestions are in fact open, clearly formulated and unambiguous commands which are easy to assimilate – e.g. Drink Coca-Cola! Choose the Better One! Relax!, You will now feel a pleasant relaxation; your body will feel heavy ... Sleep!, etc.

The important thing about direct suggestions is that they must be short, to the point, simple, and not negative in content – i.e. they must not contain a negative expression like the word "no" – because, as we said earlier, only the conscious mind operates with negative concepts, whereas we are trying to communicate with the subconscious. In this case the nonverbal behaviour is likewise authoritarian and must intensify the effect achieved by words – the hypnotist might choose a position slightly higher than that of the subject; he or she might try to invade a part of the subject's personal space; his or her gestures might become imperative, his or her voice more authoritative, etc.

Naturally, we cannot use direct suggestions in every single case, and that is why we need to know when they might be effective. First and foremost, we must say that the more alert and vigilant the conscious mind of the person we want to hypnotise is, the more inadequate the use of direct suggestions will be. In addition, many people are inclined to resist direct commands. That is why it is safe and effective to use open and direct suggestions when the subject is in deep or at least medium trance – i.e. when the potential of the conscious is limited.

For their part, indirect suggestions address the subconscious. Actually, as noted above, our purpose is to avoid the critical faculty of the conscious, to bypass it and to communicate directly with the subconscious, where we can validate our formulations.

Indirect suggestions are in principle quite fluid and variable, and depend on the individual situation. Notably, nonverbal communication plays a much more important role in them. To cite a good example of nonverbal individual suggestion: while talking about particular sensations in the arm of a man we want to hypnotise, all we have to do is adjust our speech tempo to his breathing rate and we will see a change – while our subject's conscious mind accepts or resists the sensations in his arm, his breathing will become synchronised with our rhythm of speech. So when we slow down, we will see his breathing slow down too. In this case we have direct access to the subject's subconscious, which responds to our indirect verbal suggestion concerning his breathing, while his conscious mind assumes that our main purpose is to produce some kind of sensation in his arm.

It is very important that every suggestion you make to the subject must be true. Truth is a very relative notion. They say that the entire art of magic is always to tell the truth – to live with the truth to such an extent that you become identical with it. In this case the truth complies with you to the extent to which you yourself comply with the truth. Thus, to achieve the desired effect of hypnotic trance, you must use the power of truth. For example, if you tell the hypnotised subject that his or her muscles are relaxed and that the slightest movement is very tiring, this must really be true; if you tell people that they are at peace, they really should be at peace. That is how you win the subject's confidence and consent. Yet to know what the real sensations of your entranced subject are, to some extent you yourself must also be in a trance while retaining control. In other words, in hypnosis *the client should be in a trance state while the hypnotist should be in a state of trance and control.*

In fact, as Milton H. Erickson says, suggestions are statements which the client cannot challenge. And since our purpose is to enhance the effectiveness of our hypnotic work, we must say that it is always safe to suggest a behaviour that is inevitably bound to follow in a natural way – for example, to suggest that subjects close their eyes when we see that they look really tired and will inevitably close their eyes themselves. It is quite another matter that it is we who are actually inducing this sense of exhaustion.

Besides, suggestions are always made in a form which the client accepts readily. A suggestion that involves an interesting experience or relaxation and pleasant inaction will be accepted much more easily than an intimidating suggestion of loss of limb control. What we should also keep in mind is that impossible suggestions do not work. We must also say a few words about posthypnotic suggestions. As the very term shows, these are suggestions of which the effect is felt after the subject emerges from hypnosis. If the subject is in deep trance, we could directly suggest to him or her that after waking he or she will experience, feel (or not feel), do (or not do), forget (or remember) something, etc. What we should always remember about direct posthypnotic suggestion is that its power usually weakens after every natural sleep state. That is why what may be really effective, especially for the purposes of psychotherapy, are indirect posthypnotic suggestions. All the more so in that the subject does not need to forget them in order to carry them out – i.e. we are not dependent on the presence or absence of amnesia. Perhaps we should note here that effectiveness does not depend on the depth of the hypnotic trance. It depends on the way in which the suggestion is conveyed to the subconscious. You could readily suggest something absurd to someone even in a full waking state.

Talking of hypnosis and suggestion, we must also mention some tests of the level of suggestibility or, more precisely, of the subject's readiness to enter a trance at a particular moment and under the prevailing circumstances. Actually, such tests are formal and standard, and they usually reveal an intention to influence the tested person in some way. What is valuable in this case is that if the result is positive, we could imperceptibly proceed from testing to hypnotic induction proper. Some of the most popular suggestibility tests are:

- The *postural sway test* is very popular. In the classic variant, the subject stands with feet together and eyes closed. Our purpose is to make them sway or topple in any direction by means of direct or indirect suggestions.
- In another popular suggestibility test, we try to cause *arm levitation or heaviness*. If we concentrate on a given part of our body, we will inevitably feel something – no matter what – in that particular part. Thus we could quite easily make someone feel that his or her arm is light or heavy.
- We could also apply the *arm attraction* test. In the popular variant, we ask the subject to stretch out the arms with palms facing each other, and start suggesting that the arms attract each other, that some force is pulling them together, etc. I am sure that you will be surprised at how effective this test is.
- The *hand-clasping and locking* test is also quite effective.
- We could also suggest *heavy eyelids leading to eye closure.*
- Since we are discussing suggestibility tests and not hypnotic induction, we will also mention *monitoring the vocabulary of the person we want to hypnotise* – is he or she using words, phrases or concepts that he or she has accepted and borrowed from us? This is a positive indicator that we already have some influence over them.

The list of tests could go on forever for the simple reason that every correct communication could give us information about the level of the other person's suggestibili, – which means that what could help us best is experience transformed into practical knowledge.

We should also remember that these are only tests designed to show us whether *this* is precisely the right moment to proceed with trance induction. If there is anything that suggests the contrary, the best option is to find an excuse to postpone the induction of hypnosis, since an initial failure would significantly lower the chance of our subsequent success with the client in question. Yet we should aspire towards success, because just as the apple tree produces apples and the peach tree produces peaches, so success produces successes, and failure failures. And if you are a novice, it would be better by far for you to avoid an unsuccessful start. That is why I suggest that before you try any of the above-mentioned tests, you be patient and wait until you have not only read but also learned about the specificity of hypnotic verbal and nonverbal communication, as expounded in the next chapters.

Chapter 4
Approaches in Hypnosis

The authoritarian (direct) approach;
The standardised approach;
The Ericksonian approach

It is extremely difficult to discuss what are described as traditional and non-traditional hypnosis in an entirely impartial way; yet if we think about it, we will realise that in fact impartiality is a virtue valued foremost by adherents of tradition – whether in hypnosis, psychotherapy or any other sphere. It is unrealistic to assume that we can jump over our own shadow or that we can consciously control all our actions or thoughts. It is just as unrealistic to think that we can avoid expressing our personal opinion in some way, hard as we might try not to. If anyone disagrees, let them exercise their impartiality while reading the following paragraphs.

Yet before we proceed to examine the polemic between the main schools, let us take a look at the major theories designed to explain hypnosis and, more precisely, the therapeutic trance. The most popular psychotherapeutic theory is undoubtedly Freud's psychoanalysis. Anyone who has studied Freud knows that he started his medical practice by applying hypnosis but soon gave it up, assuming that hypnosis was inapplicable to the majority of patients – at that time it was believed that very few people could be put into a trance. Either way, however, trance states undoubtedly play a crucial role in any form of psychotherapy – irrespective of whether they are deliberately induced or spontaneous as in everyday life. If we consider the tenets of the Freudian *psychodynamic theory* on the nature of trance, we will note that according to this theory a strong relationship develops between the client and the hypnotist in the hypnotic process, and the client shifts to a less analytical and more primary information-processing level.

There is also what is known as *learning theory*, which holds that trance is a naturalistic skill that can be learned, and that hypnotisability can be improved with practice.

According to the *neo-dissociation theory*, hypnotised individuals are often dissociated from normal monitoring and control processes, and this general dissociation permits the development of specific dissociational phenomena such as age regression, hallucinations, amnesia and anaesthesia. It is also assumed that dissociative experiences can occur in other similar states such as contemplation, daydreaming and meditation.

Also interesting is *role-playing theory*, which claims that hypnosis and trance are really just metaphors and should not be reified, or in other words, what happens under hypnosis is actually unconscious role-playing on the part of the hypnotised subject (he or she does not have amnesia but plays the role of someone who does have amnesia, etc.). In addition, this theory assumes that because trance is a response occurring within a social psychological context, situational variables must always be taken into account (e.g. the nature of the relationship established with the hypnotist – an unconscious desire to "please" the hypnotist, to show off, etc.).

For its part, *motivated involvement theory* claims that trance is a naturalistic experience that is phenomenologically similar to other psychological experiences, and therefore that any willing subject can be trained to go into a trance. In addition, it is considered that formal inductions and rituals are not needed for hypnosis. According to the adherents of this theory, developing good rapport with, adequately informing, and effectively motivating the client is both necessary and fundamental.

In fact, each one of these theories is valid at a particular time and in a particular context. That is why we should seek a unifying theory that explains things and that is applicable in practice to the fullest possible extent. In this respect, there are three main rival concepts in modern hypnosis: the authoritarian (traditional), the standardised (experimental) and the Ericksonian (non-traditional) approaches.

We will examine each of these schools of thought from various aspects and try to answer the question, "Which one of these approaches would be not only the most effective but also the most universally applicable?"

We can safely say that the age of the common application of *authoritarian hypnosis* in clinical practice is, if not over, then at least drawing to an end. Today this type of hypnotic influence is applied mainly in the form of stage hypnosis in entertainment establishments. That is because the main purpose of all authoritarian behaviour is usually to impress the audience and thus impose the will of the hypnotist, who is the main factor and central figure in the whole process. In this case we can hardly talk of communication on an equal footing because suggestions are given in the form of direct commands, while the subject's task is usually to carry them out, so exhibiting unusual and strange behaviour.

For the same reason – to impress onlookers and to win their cooperation – authoritarian hypnosis prefers quick and spectacular induction techniques. When the hypnotised subject responds as required, champions of the standard authoritarian approach say that he or she is obeying the hypnotist's commands. In the opposite case they assume that the subject is resisting. I think that this kind of interpretation is too categorical, and that it is more appropriate to the exact sciences than to such a controversial subject as trance and trance processes.

Things are quite different in the case of the *standardised approach* in hypnosis, which is also best suited to conducting experiments. This, in its turn, makes it a reliable method of the serious and systematic theoretical study of hypnosis. The standardised approach is therefore applied, for the most part, under laboratory conditions for the purpose of exploring various phenomena typical of the hypnotic state. Unlike authoritarian hypnosis, the main factor in this type of hypnotic process is the hypnotised subject, who is influenced with the help of what are assumed to be universal techniques and standard suggestions. The hypnotised subject's main task is to follow the hypnotist's instructions as precisely as possible. If the subject complies with the hypnotist's suggestions, adherents to this approach say that the subject is hypnotisable. In the opposite case they assume that he or she is not susceptible to hypnotic influence.

It must be noted that this approach is entirely free of the mystic aura of hypnosis and normally does not strive to achieve a spectacular effect. Nonetheless, the focus is on the hypnotised subject's behaviour and responses, which by themselves alone provide the information necessary for the construction of a theoretical framework.

The standardised approach to hypnosis would undoubtedly and thoroughly satisfy the intellectual and practical pursuits of anyone who has a classical mindset and an academic background.

Things are entirely different in the case of *Ericksonian hypnosis*, which is regarded as a non-traditional method and applied foremost in clinical practice and psychotherapy. In this situational context, the main purpose is to create favourable conditions for achieving the required therapeutic changes in the individual patient's or client's thinking, perceptions, value system and behaviour.

Ericksonian hypnosis differs significantly from the other two approaches described above. It gives priority to the therapeutic process itself, in which the hypnotist's influence is neither direct nor standard but extremely flexible and adjustable to the individual traits of the subject. That is precisely why it uses mainly indirect and concealed suggestions and communications, which unobtrusively help the subject do his or her part of the job. And if in the authoritarian and standardised approaches our task is to make the subject act unusually or simply carry out our commands, here our purpose is to enable the subject to encounter intimate inner sensations and experiences in the context of a safe therapeutic relationship.

In Ericksonian hypnosis the duration of hypnotic induction usually varies even in the case of a single subject, because the preparations for trance induction are in themselves part of the therapeutic and hypnotic process.

The subject's behaviour is also interpreted in a different way. Every hypnotic response is assumed to result from the subconscious choice of a client who is responding in the way that is most appropriate for him or her.

On the other hand, the client's "non-hypnotic" behaviour is regarded as a source of unconsciously provided information about additional factors that the hypnotist should take into consideration in order to achieve the desired trance state.

In addition, we should note that this method is concerned primarily with the client's inner sensations and the subsequent change in his or her behavioural model.

Perhaps it would be also useful to note several main principles in Ericksonian hypnosis which highlight the difference between it and the authoritarian and standardised approaches.

- The main postulate of the Ericksonian school is that every individual is unique and that the approach to each person should be tailored to accommodate this uniqueness.
- Clinical hypnosis and therapeutic trance (if we use those terms as synonyms) are assumed to be nothing but a precisely planned continuation of certain everyday processes in normal life.
- Trance has a therapeutic effect in itself, because we all have productive resources and an ability to enter a trance state under appropriate circumstances, and the trance state specifically activates those resources.
- Direct suggestions are likely to cause direct resistance. That is why it is so necessary to find indirect ways of accessing the client's subconscious mind.
- Accurate communication is the basis of hypnotic induction. Everything else is of secondary importance.

Everything noted above might lead readers to the justified conclusion that there are two, and not three, schools – hypnosis and Ericksonian hypnosis. And that would not be far from the truth. Yet they would be even closer to the truth if they assumed something else – that Ericksonian hypnosis is *not* a different current, school or approach. In fact, it is the quintessence – the highest form of the art of hypnosis – the natural result of more than 200 years of improvement in hypnotic techniques and the application of the therapeutic trance. In terms of the contemporary level of development of hypnosis in the world, a practical mastery and understanding of the principles of Ericksonian hypnosis is the highest achievement in this field of knowledge, since it cannot be attained unless the authoritarian and standardised approaches have been mastered first. So for anyone to assume that it is possible to skip the other two approaches and proceed straight to Ericksonian hypnosis is a big mistake. As is to ignore and underrate the Ericksonian approach. For we must not forget that our ultimate purpose is maximum effectiveness in our work with trance.

Our ultimate purpose in any sphere of life – consciously or not – is knowledge and ability. As the prominent Bulgarian writer Nikolai Haitov puts it, "It is one thing to know, another to be able to, and yet another to actually do something." Yet we sometimes forget the main factor that determines our success along the path to knowledge – we forget our moral self-improvement. Especially if we consider the fact that in practising hypnosis we are responsible not only for ourselves but also for the person who – rightly or wrongly – has placed his or her trust in us and allowed us into the most intimate and nebulous realm of his or her unique essence. And all too often this selfsame person is unaware of the huge risk he or she has taken. Even worse, we as hypnotists are sometimes not aware either. And that is precisely the reason for including the next chapter, which can be skipped by all who regard it as unimportant.

Chapter 5
On Ability and Knowledge

This is not a sermon. Nor is it a superficial attempt to bulk up the size of this book. Actually, I would have preferred to avoid this subject altogether. It is like a jungle full of dangers and predators. I seriously doubt that I can get through it unscathed – but if one really wants to understand whether this is the right path, one must be prepared to close one's eyes and walk in the dark.

This chapter is not simply necessary. It is essential. It is compulsory reading because – unfortunately – in all the books and films and disks and media articles on hypnosis and on training in hypnosis, priority is given mainly to various schools, approaches, techniques, methods, principles, and so forth. Well, of course those things do have to be studied in detail – and that, indeed, is why you will find them in the subsequent chapters of this book. Yet sometimes people can concentrate on them too much and so miss the most important step in mastering not only hypnosis but any other practical aspect of knowledge – namely, purposeful and continuous work on one's own spiritual (moral, emotional, intellectual) and physical (as you know, the two are inseparable) self-improvement.

I am sure we all agree that this is a cliché, a truth that has become banal. The bad thing is that we are increasingly shifting the emphasis from its truth to its banality. Otherwise, we would have to seriously commit ourselves to self-improvement Yet that requires considerable effort – discipline, patience, occasional privations and risks, frequent disappointments, while keeping up a constant quest for new challenges. It may sound stupid to some and romantic to others – but either way, it sounds so probably because it is a kind of terra incognita which not all people dare explore. And this applies to many of us because it is "all too human" to choose the easier way.

It is easier to give than to follow advice.

It is easier, for example, to set than to keep a diet or any other regime. ("I will definitely start tomorrow. Or better, leave it for Monday.")

It is easier to find an excuse for a bad habit than to give it up. ("I smoke because I have problems.")

It is easier to follow a well-trodden path than to blaze a trail.

It is easier to renounce and ridicule than to try to grasp things you do not understand. ("What? The Earth's supposed to be *round*? Nonsense!").

It is easier to get to know others than to get to know yourself.

And it is easier to become faultless in hypnotic techniques or in any other skills than to become faultless in your own character.

Yet the easy way is not the right way if you are seeking total mastery in this (or any other) field – mastery that equates not so much to skill as to an art.

It is a main postulate that if you want to turn a particular knowledge or skill into an art, you must make sure that your work reflects your inner world. But whereas in painting, music, poetry or dance you can afford to express your fears, nightmares and madness along with cosmological beauty and harmony, in hypnosis – especially in therapy – it is inconceivable and unpardonable to offer your own weaknesses and chaos to a person who has turned to you for help. If you do, you will only end up wondering why the reliable techniques you have strictly observed are failing to produce the effect they are supposed to. And it is easier to blame the techniques than yourself. Or to renounce hypnosis altogether.

In discussing self-knowledge and therapy, I certainly do not mean to endorse the psychodynamic theory, which requires future therapists to undergo therapy themselves for years. Nor do I mean to denigrate it. It should be noted, however, that such therapy is only one of the many ways to learn more about our inner selves, and that it is a way suitable mainly for those who have found their answers in the Freudian concept of human nature.

If, then, we can put aside such a fanatical attitude to psychoanalysis or to any other theory, we will realise that there are indeed other ways to improve our self-knowledge and to develop and strengthen the inner integrity, power and harmony that are so essential for the therapeutic process. Unless we do that for ourselves, it is unrealistic to hope that we can do it for others. How can somebody else rely on you if you yourself cannot? It is difficult to believe in the success and future possibilities of the person opposite you if you do not believe in your own success and future possibilities. Yet without faith, to quote a prominent writer, the cross remains nothing but two crossed sticks.

Some might now be wondering which are the other ways – apart from personal analysis and therapy – to gain knowledge of the self, of one's own weaknesses, of one's unsuspected resources of strength, of one's unacknowledged hopes, of the promises made to oneself in early childhood, etc.

As I see it, the ways number around 6 billion and are increasing steadily, if UN statistics are to be trusted. Every single one of us has his or her own unique way in which he or she must pass the time assigned to him or her on Earth, and every single one of us learns in his or her individual way things about himself or herself, about others, and about the nature of the surrounding world.

We can learn from our family.

We can learn from a particular person who has a special role in our life.

We can learn from a university or another educational establishment or community.

We can learn from our profession.

We can learn from our hobbies.

We can learn from some personal misfortune followed by good fortune.

We can learn from some personal good fortune, followed by misfortune.

We can learn from the God we believe in.

We can learn from our favourite poet, writer, artist, composer or actor.

We can learn from everything – as the woodcarver learns from wood, the sculptor from stone, the gardener from a plant, the mother from the child, the warrior from his foe, the doctor from the patient, the shaman from the spirit, and all of us from life.

In other words, life experience can be acquired in the psychiatrist's consulting room or at the university in Oxford, just as anywhere else. In *Zen and the Art of Motorcycle Maintenance*, Robert M. Pirsig writes:

> The Buddha, the Godhead, resides quite as comfortably in ... the gears of a [motor]cycle transmission as he does at the top of a mountain or in the petals of a flower. To think otherwise is to demean the Buddha – which is to demean oneself.

In the same way, any truth, known or unknown, either is all around us or is not at all. So the question is not where but *how* to find it. Yes, each one of us has his or her own way, but all too often the obstacles and enemies we encounter along our way are the same for all of us. Perhaps you will agree that in general our greatest handicaps are fear and the sense of self-importance. Naturally, I have in mind the unhealthy manifestation of both. For there is a difference between reasonable caution and debilitating fear, just as there is a difference between healthy self-respect and dignity, and obsessive personal ambition and selfishness.

If we now examine these two most common pitfalls along the path to knowledge and ability, we ought to start with the feeling of self-importance and personal ambition, because fear is far less often the motivation behind any sort of quest.

The desire to bolster the importance of our own self can take many forms: ruthless professional ambition, populism, unscrupulousness, intolerance for other people's opinions, an undiscriminating attitude to everything that confirms our greatness, and, most frequently, outward manifestations of self-love.

Some may be wondering what this has to do with hypnosis. It has a lot to do with it, I would say – because the relationship between hypnotist and client is very personal and strongly intuitive, and in this context our clients can "feel us out" perfectly well. If we have succeeded in coming close enough to them, their subconsciouses are entirely capable of identifying the negative overtones of our intentions in approaching them, and that reduces the efficiency of our work. It would be wonderful if we managed to turn our professional ambitions into a sincere interest in our work; to turn cheap populism into an ability to communicate in simple and comprehensible terms; to turn unscrupulousness into an ability to uphold our personal convictions in a worthy way; to turn intolerance into progressive thinking; and so on. Believe me: the more are our victories over this enemy, the greater are our chances of being "liked" by the subconscious of the person we want to hypnotise.

But there is something else. Hypnotists are all too often regarded as people who have all but unlocked the innermost human and esoteric secrets, and who have power over other people's destiny. Perhaps this attitude is due to the mystery and mystique that surround hypnosis – caused, inevitably, by what is for the conscious mind the incomprehensible way in which the subconscious works. In any case it is very tempting to present yourself in the eyes of people who are less informed or who are influenced by you as a master of supernatural forces, as a guru, as God's Chosen One, or as an omnipotent healer or omniscient sage and magus. Those who want to present themselves in this way are simply wasting their time on this book, however, because it deals only with all sorts of questions related to hypnosis and hypnotherapy. Admittedly, there is very much in common between therapy and various religious and esoteric practices, but there is very little in common between therapists and quack "masters of science" fighting tooth and nail to win some scientific or popular halo. I am reminded of a Japanese treatise called *Zen and the Art of Archery*, which says, among other things:

> The good archer takes aim above all at himself.

And because I would not wish to underestimate your intelligence, dear reader, by going any further into this matter, I will now say something about fear too – the enemy that we all inevitably encounter at the beginning of our road. I cannot tell you anything truer about fear than what has already been written by Carlos Castaneda – the person who has changed the worldview of more than one generation of spirit seekers. So I will quote an excerpt from his book *The Teaching of Don Juan*.

"When a man starts to learn, he is never clear about his objectives. His purpose is faulty; his intent is vague. He hopes for rewards that will never materialize, for he knows nothing of the hardships of learning.

"He slowly begins to learn – bit by bit at first, that in big chunks. And his thoughts soon clash. What he learns is never what he pictured or imagined, and so he begins to be afraid. Learning is never what one expects. Every step of the learning is a new task, and the fear the man is experiencing begins to mount mercilessly, unyieldingly. His purpose becomes a battlefield.

"And thus he has tumbled upon the first of his natural enemies: Fear! A terrible enemy – treacherous, and difficult to overcome. It remains concealed at every turn of the way, prowling, waiting. And if the man, terrified in its presence, runs away, his enemy will have put an end to his quest.

"What will happen to the man if he runs away in fear?

"Nothing happens to him except that he will never learn. He will never become a man of knowledge. He will perhaps be a bully or a harmless, scared man; at any rate he will be a defeated man. His first enemy will have put an end to his cravings"

What a wonderful way of putting it! I don't think I can add anything – except perhaps to address those who think I am exaggerating and persuade them that if there is any one area in which they are sooner or later bound to face something scary and unclear, that area is precisely hypnosis.

The ancient Greeks said that knowledge is like a torch you carry on your back – it lights up the path of those who follow. And if we want to explore hitherto unknown areas, we must consciously take the risk of experimenting, because sometimes instead of looking for the footprints of our predecessors, it is better if we go seeking what they sought for too.

Arguably, there are three zones we could explore on our cognitive and spiritual journey – the known (what we already know); the unknown that is, however, knowable; and the unknowable. Reason – i.e. the conscious mind – can naturally reach only the first two zones, but the trance state often contains elements that belong to the third one, the unknowable. And if we are unprepared for such an encounter, there is a very real danger that we might bring chaos and destruction not only to our client's psyche but also to our own. In that case we would be totally undermined, just as we would be in the opposite case – when fear paralyses us and compels us to give up our intentions. All fear can do is scare (but it can do it sometimes to death), and the most secure and effective weapon we have against it is self-knowledge and a readiness to take responsibility for the decisions we make on the basis of that knowledge. This is also the best guarantee for the security of the person who has entrusted us with his or her mental health.

Things are not really that sinister, and one of the best things for us in this case is to know our own pace of mastering hypnotic theory and skills. As the founder of Taoism, Lao-Tzu, wrote more than 25 centuries ago (translated by Chad Hansen):

> Those who tiptoe do not stand.
> Those who stride do not walk.
> Those who see for themselves are not discerning.

This is a universal principle, and it naturally applies to hypnosis too – and even more to any form of therapy.

Nearing the end of this digression from the main conceptual path of this book, let us conclude by associating it with our main subject, noting expressly that true hypnotism is not a constant enrichment of the repertoire of induction techniques (that is the easy part) or the acquisition of the ability to influence other people's perceptions and behaviour. True hypnotism is neither a hobby nor a profession. True hypnotism helps those who pursue it to achieve self-realisation. True hypnotism is a way of life that transforms the practitioner almost alchemically into a constantly evolving personality who exercises a positive influence (even unconsciously) on the people around him or her. True hypnotism is not an end but a means that helps us become better.

But isn't this potentially true of everything?

Chapter 6
The Essence of Hypnotic Communication

What is communication?; Communication channels; Nonverbal communication; The language of hypnosis

If we must put forward yet another definition of hypnosis, we could say that hypnosis is a specific type of communication in which the hypnotist influences the senses of the hypnotised subject, thus altering his or her perception of the surrounding world. The important point here is that we have a *specific form of communication*. In very general terms, communication is an exchange of information. In relation to that specific form of communication, however, what part of the transmitted information we will assimilate is quite unspecific, and even more unspecific is whether we interpret it correctly. In fact, well-transmitted information does not need to be interpreted – i.e. the message reaches us without being diffracted by the individual prism of our consciousness, and takes its place in our inner world in the form of indisputable knowledge.

The hypnotist's job largely consists, first, of collecting as much information as possible about the client's immediate state, and second, of responding adequately to that information. In the course of this process, however, we should not forget the purpose we have set out to achieve – namely, to put the client into a trance.

Everything therefore starts with careful observation and an inspection for trance indicators, our main purpose being to occupy the client's complete attention. This is of paramount importance. If we capture the client's attention, we can steer his or her perceptions in any direction – just as we might control a dog on a lead. Unless we secure our client's attention, on the other hand, there is no point in trying to hypnotise him or her. It is pointless to try to work with somebody who is fidgeting nervously, for instance, because he or she is thus actually telling us that he or she is not yet ready to enter hypnosis. How to recognise the precise moment at which we have the best chance to succeed in putting the client into a trance is difficult to describe – but it is a very specific feeling, which develops with practice over time.

We must note especially that every single one of us can focus our attention on a single subject or situation – a particular book, film, conversation, or whatever. The rational mind can concentrate on one specific sphere, remaining oblivious to everything else. This is the principle of monoideism mentioned earlier. Such concentration is even easier to achieve if there is appropriate motivation

– e.g. to solve a particular problem. If while observing the subject we detect even a single indicator that he or she is in a trance – even a very light trance – we have a relatively solid basis for endeavouring to go on to deepen the trance state. Milton Erickson says that normally *the trance begins the moment we start talking about any hypnotic phenomenon that the subject is experiencing.*

So if we decide that we can proceed to induce hypnosis, we should start by *aligning* ourselves with the person we want to hypnotise. Our purpose is to achieve a kind of harmony with the client, to synchronise our rhythm with his or hers. This is usually the most effective beginning in hypnotic induction – first to align ourselves with our client – and only thereafter to start setting the rhythm and guiding the entire process in an effort to induce a trance state.

The first step is to align our behaviour with the subject's, taking into account the subject's body posture, movements, breathing rate, eye-blink frequency, speech tempo, etc. For example, we can start by mirroring – i.e. by positioning ourselves in the same posture and, at the same time, nodding whenever they breathe in or out. Or while synchronising our speech tempo with the subject's breathing rate, we can change our posture whenever the subject changes his or her. And so on. There are countless variants.

Aligning ourselves with our clients certainly does not mean that we must imitate them directly, since that can be noticed easily and will put them on their guard. We must simply adjust our rhythm to theirs and attain some kind of unity and harmony because, as noted above, hypnotism is interaction and not counteraction.

Assuming then that we have already established a stable relationship and rapport with our client in the way described above, we can proceed to lead him or her into a trance. The easiest way is to suggest that he or she experience and feel something that appeals to him or her and that he or she would enjoy. After all, it is usually easier to get something from someone if, so to speak, we promise to reward them rather than threaten to punish them. In the first case we evoke cooperation, and in the second, antagonism. This is something we must understand well, because it is an important principle in interpersonal relationships and successful communication with other people.

I should also point out that starting off with our client's mindset, and not with our own, is a basic rule in hypnotic communication. It is much more effective and easy to use mental constructs that already exist in the client's mind than to require the client to come up with new ones or to accept our own conceptual system instead. Besides, it is simpler and more effective to induce a trance and give suggestions to which the client responds by using his or her own words and experiences, since it is precisely they, along with the related mind-images, that have true value – especially in the case of therapy.

Consequently, it is also very important to use the language of our clients instead of compelling them to accept the meaning that we ourselves ascribe to words. In this respect it is very helpful to use truisms and generalities that would sound right to everyone. For example: "Everyone needs to relax and rest"; "It is nice to have nothing to worry about and to simply sit still without having to move"; and so forth. The more we speak in generalities, the smaller is the chance that our message may be mistaken. A concrete statement is much more likely to cause contradiction or a misunderstanding and thus hinder induction.

Things are entirely different in the case of communication when the subject is in a deeper hypnotic trance. Here we should keep in mind that in a deep trance state the subconscious takes everything literally. We should therefore concentrate very carefully on the absolutely literal phraseology of our verbal communications.

We could also generalise by noting that hypnotic communication should be purposive but not intrusive, persuasive but not intimidating, guiding but not compelling, and natural but not elementary. In the same context, the hypnotist's verbal behaviour should be in harmony with the nonverbal, but without stimulating undue interest. It should convey a sense of relaxation but not boredom; it should be confident but not arrogant, it should be attractive but not embarrassing, and it should express the full competence of what occurs during the hypnotic trance.

With reference to successful communication in terms of the effective input and output of information, we should also note one of Milton Erickson's discoveries, expounded in detail by his followers and students John Grinder and Richard Bandler, the inventors of neuro-linguistic programming (NLP). They state that eye movements, or "eye accessing cues", give an indication of an individual's way of thinking or, more precisely, of the way in which he or she processes information and turns it into personal inner experience. Observing eye movements can tell us a lot about what is happening in our client's inner world. If we ask someone a question that requires consideration, we will detect a change in his or her line of sight. This change can give us an accurate indication of the way in which the person is processing the information received.

If we ask people a question that compels them to use their visual memory – e.g. "What colour were the shoes of your partner at your senior prom?" "When did you last see your friend?" – along with the verbal response we will also get the eye movement pattern typical of the visual memory: *eyes up and left.*

In response to our suggestion that they construct a visual image, i.e. imagine something that they have never seen – e.g. a pink elephant with horns, or what they would look like in five years' time – the person will move his or her *eyes up and right.*

If the person has to answer a question concerning auditory memory – e.g. "What does your father's voice sound like?" "How does your clock sound its alarm?" – we will detect a *lateral left eye movement.*

When someone has to come up with an auditory construct, looking for an answer to such questions as, "How would your voice sound if you had a pail over your head?" "How would a large pot falling to the ground from the sixth floor sound?", his or her eyes will *move laterally to the right.*

The use of kinaesthetic experience – motor, tactile, thermal, gustatory, olfactory memory – is associated with an eye movement *down and to the right.*

It is worth noting that it is impossible for us to create kinaesthetic constructs – i.e. we cannot imagine what something we have never felt before feels like. This is an extremely interesting fact which confirms the thesis that our eyes and ears can be "taught" to see and hear – unlike our sense of smell, taste and touch, which remain primary and original, and perceive the world around us in a way that impacts foremost on our subconscious. On the other hand, our sight and hearing depend on the evolution of the conscious mind. We thus have every grounds for asking ourselves a question that tends towards implications of the philosophical: could every visual and auditory piece of information be some kind of construct "taught" to us by the community we live in? If we reason along these lines, we will probably arrive at the concept of the illusory nature of the physical world, as propounded by almost all religions and idealistic philosophical schools. However, further inquiry into this question would represent a digression from our specific subject, and so we will continue exploring the link between eye movements and cognitive processing.

Next comes the movement of the eyes *down and left*, which indicates that the person is engaged in internal dialogue. This eye movement is also an indicator of speech control, when people are picking their words carefully – e.g. as in an interview, in interpreting from another language or when reporting.

So the three main ways of receiving and processing information that are relevant to us are the visual, the auditory and the kinaesthetic. We use all three, but every one of us has one particular way that is dominant. Observing eye movements is one of the tools that helps us identify our clients' – or our partner's – dominant system.

Those who are visually-oriented may consult *Figure 1*, which shows the link between cognitive processing and eye movements.

Figure 1

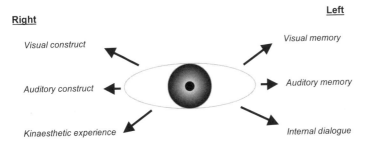

Right

Left

Visual construct

Visual memory

Auditory construct

Auditory memory

Kinaesthetic experience

Internal dialogue

Bear in mind, however, that left-handed people tend to be reversed from left to right – i.e. their eye accessing cues are the mirror-image of those of the average right-hander, since this has to do with the workings of the brain.

Yet observing our partner's or our clients' eye movements is not the only way we can identify their dominant sensory perception system. If we listen carefully to what they are saying, we may find that the actual words they use can also give us a good idea of their sensory type.

People with dominant visual perception frequently use such words as "dark", "light", "clear" and "picture", and expressions like "I tend to *see* things in *black and white*," "I can't *see* a way out of this situation," "I *see clearly* what you mean," "The *picture* doesn't *look* very *rosy*" and "I don't *see light* at the end of the tunnel."

Auditory-oriented people often use words like "speak", "hear", "listen", "loud" and "ring", and expressions like "That doesn't *sound* too good," "That *rings a bell*," "I *told* myself that it doesn't really matter what people were *saying* about me," and "The facts *screamed* at me."

Kinaesthetically-oriented people tend to discuss matters in terms such as "heavy", "light", "warm", "cold", "hard", "soft", "narrow", "broad", and so on, saying things like "It's been a *heavy* day," "The news sent *shivers down my spine*," "I don't want to have the authorities *breathing down my neck*," "I was *paralysed* with fear," "I have a *lump in my throat*," "I can't go round with the *burdens* of the world on my *shoulders* all the time," "A great *weight lifted* from me" and "How *sweet* of you to think of me."

Some may wonder whether we really need to go into such details. The answer is that this knowledge is a significant prerequisite for successful communication. For example, it would be much more difficult for us to get our message across to someone who is visually-oriented if we suggest that they *feel* or *hear* something, in that it is much easier for them to *see* what we really mean. In other words, if we use the same language as our client, we have a better chance of communicating with him or her – especially considering that *we* are in the role of the person who is supposed to know how to achieve that.

We must realise that to improve our communications skills, which are fundamental to effective hypnotism and psychotherapy, is impossible without determined effort. The habit of observing the behavioural characteristics, eye movements and speech of our clients is perhaps the most important and indispensable exercise to include in our learning or self-training in hypnosis.

In sum, eye movements and customary modes of verbal expression give us valuable information about the client or subject we want to hypnotise. At the same time, however, we need channels by which to communicate information that will help us influence the outward behaviour and inner experiences of the person opposite us. Because verbal expression is censored much more strictly by the conscious mind, it is much more expedient for us to look for nonverbal communication channels to give us more direct and imperceptible access to the subconscious. The main parameters of behaviour that can be used as channels of a nonverbal exchange of information include body posture, breathing rate, speech tempo, intonation, facial expression, body movements, and the eye-blink frequency.

In order to present the principles of nonverbal communication in an understandable way, I will refer to the diagrammatic framework put forward by one of the best researchers in the field of hypnosis, Steven Gilligan, in his excellent book *Therapeutic Trances*.

One of the ways to align with our subject and "tune in" to those channels of communication is full and direct mirroring, which means aligning as many parameters of our behaviour as possible with those of our client's. For example, we adopt the same posture, breathe at the same rate, use the client's intonation and speech tempo, imitate the client's facial expression, make the same body movements, and so on. This process is illustrated in *Figure 2* below.

Figure 2

Hypnotist's behaviour		Hypnotised subject's behaviour
Body posture	⟶	Body posture
Breathing rate	⟶	Breathing rate
Speech tempo	⟶	Speech tempo
Intonation	⟶	Intonation
Facial expression	⟶	Facial expression
Body movements	⟶	Body movements
Eye-blink frequency	⟶	Eye-blink frequency
Others	⟶	Others

This kind of mirroring, however, is not particularly productive in practice for two main reasons: first, it is very difficult and demanding to mirror your client fully; and second, it cannot be discreet enough to escape the attention of the conscious mind. By applying this method we will, in all likelihood, put clients on their guard. That is why *partial and direct mirroring and alignment* is preferable. In this case we choose only two or three of the more important and imperceptible behaviour parameters of our client and synchronise directly with them. For example, we might mirror only their breathing rate, speech tempo and body movements, as shown in *Figure 3*.

Figure 3

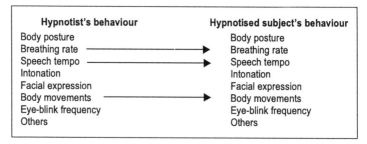

But without doubt the most convenient, effective and feasible variant is *partial indirect alignment*. This, however, requires exceptional alertness, ingenuity and concentration of attention – because it is certainly not easy, say, to align your speech tempo with your client's breathing rate while marking with supposedly random movements of your body the changes in his or her speech tempo, and using your intonation to note the changes in his or her facial expression. I am sure that this sounds confusing, so I hope my point is made in *Figure 4 below*.

Figure 4

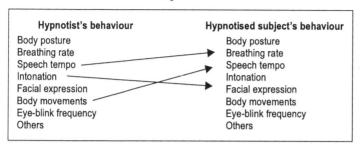

Hypnotist's behaviour	Hypnotised subject's behaviour
Body posture	Body posture
Breathing rate	Breathing rate
Speech tempo	Speech tempo
Intonation	Intonation
Facial expression	Facial expression
Body movements	Body movements
Eye-blink frequency	Eye-blink frequency
Others	Others

Needless to say, the variants in pacing our subject's nonverbal behaviour are countless. We therefore need to choose and master several only. In this way we can make a beginning from which to expand our arsenal of techniques that influence the behaviour and hence the perceptions of our clients. And since we are discussing nonverbal communication, let us conclude here by stressing that the best teacher in this case is again practical experience.

As noted above, in our everyday contacts with people we normally try to choose our words and lend them the precise meaning we want to convey. It is much harder, however, to control nonverbal communication to the same extent. In other words, important as exactly *what* we say might be, it is much more important *how* we say it. Of course, this principle is especially important in such a specific and intensive form of communication as hypnotism. Let us repeat that hypnotism in itself is a method of control – control over the behaviour and inner processes of the hypnotised individual, but above all control over our own behaviour and emotional state. You cannot expect someone to be at ease if you yourself are nervous and anxious.

Nonverbal communication involves not only the indications or cues *we* give the person we want to hypnotise but also the cues *they* give us. Because trance is characterised by motor inhibition – normally a person in a state of trance is disinclined to move, and therefore even the slightest body movement is of special importance – we must observe every single change in facial expression and body movement very carefully. For example, what might seem an involuntary nod might tell us that the hypnotised person agrees with us. Or if a client is age-regressed we might detect a visible change in facial tension and the assumption of a childlike expression – an indication that we have established rapport and that our suggestions are working.

Occasionally, a hypnotised client may demand something – perhaps to remain longer in the trance state or, conversely, to wake up; to avoid some suggested situation – to change posture, say, or to do something that is impossible until it is suggested to him or her; etc. In such cases it is normal to observe strange and unusual behaviour in the client that has nothing to do with anything we have suggested – trembling, faster breathing, attempts to speak or move, an intense facial expression, etc. – even, but very rarely, spontaneous emergence from the trance state. In short, those *prima facie* spontaneous and random movements might express the hypnotised person's wishes or needs.

I remember a demonstration in which a 13-year-old boy in deep hypnosis suddenly started trembling all over without any visible cause. This upset and even frightened some of the participants in the seminar. The only thing that was obvious to me was that the boy wanted to tell me something. But because he was in a deep trance he could not do what he wanted unless he acted against my suggestions, which did not include waking up or doing anything without my direction. So his subconscious had chosen to remain in a trance, but to attract my attention by this physical reaction. Much to the relief of those who were frightened, it turned out that the boy simply needed to go to the toilet and conveyed this to me without disrupting our rapport.

Talking of rapport, let us note that we may establish two-way communication with the hypnotised person by using the ideomotor aspect of the trance state – in other words, we can ask clients to respond via nonverbal cues. For example, we might suggest that they respond to our questions or expectations by moving the finger of one hand for "yes", and of the other for "no". In fact, we can "impose" any nonverbal cue we want to, but we must keep in mind that the easier it is to perform, the more spontaneous our client's response will be. And we must also remember that a non-response might also be an effective response.

Either way, it is impossible to describe nonverbal communication in full because it is impossible to cover its infinite aspects. The only way we might gain some real control in this sphere is therefore by means of meticulously careful observation and practice, which in time help us gradually to develop a "gut feeling" for nonverbal communication.

Someone once said that the only way to develop our sixth sense was by perfecting the other five. By this logic, nonverbal communication must be practised rather than discussed. We will have made a significant step forward if we have become accustomed to asking ourselves the question, "Does my behaviour right now convey what I mean?" Simple as this might sound, it will focus our attention on that question and enable us to develop a habit that is extremely helpful even in everyday communication.

You could practise in the pub, for example. Pick a table with several people, observe them carefully, and try to guess when they are about to leave. Try to guess who will be the first to get up.

Or while talking with someone, casually tap your fingers in tune with their breathing rate. You will be amazed that after just a couple of minutes, his or her breathing rate will change when you change the rhythm of your tapping.

In other words, if we know the theoretical framework of nonverbal communication, all we need is determination, persistence and imagination to make progress in this field.

Now let us move on to verbal communication and consider the language of hypnotism. If we recall the direct, authoritarian way of hypnotism and suggestion, we see that the verbal communications applied are typically short, clear, unambiguous and simple, since the purpose is immediate and unconditional comprehension. Negatives are avoided whenever possible, because only the conscious mind operates with negative notions whereas our purpose is to communicate with the subconscious.

Communications in direct authoritarian suggestion are commands, which are more effective if they start with a verb in the imperative: "Raise your arm!" "Lean backwards!" "Sleep deeply!" "Drink Coca-Cola!" As noted above, in general it is safest to use direct suggestions when the subject is in deep hypnosis because we can bypass the critical faculty of the conscious mind.

Things are entirely different in the case of indirect suggestions, which might sometimes be much like a game of chess. Indirect suggestions are complex sentences made up of several different messages. Part of those messages is addressed to the conscious mind for various purposes: to confuse it, to distract it, to win its consent, etc. In themselves they constitute *alignment* (referred to hereafter as **A**) with the situational context and the behaviour of the subject.

The other kind of messages is constituted by the *suggestions* (**S**) we want to pass "unhindered" to the subconscious mind. This means that our purpose is to avoid, bypass, "sneak past" the censorship of the conscious mind, thus implanting those suggestions in the fertile soil of the subconscious, which has a far greater potential than the supposedly dominant conscious mind. Let us briefly examine several major models of phrasing indirect suggestions, again using Steven Gilligan's theoretical framework.

One major model of phrasing a suggestion in a way that conditions the client to be responsive might be, for example, **A** *and* **A** *and* **A** *and* **A** *and* **A** *and* **S**, as in:

1) You are now sitting in this chair   **A**
2) and looking straight ahead,   **A**
3) and you can hear the sounds all around,   **A**
4) and listen to my voice,   **A**

5) and you notice how A
6) steady your breathing has become. S

What are we actually doing in this case? With the first five parts of this sentence we are aligning with the situation of the other person – namely, what his or her real kinaesthetic, visual and auditory perceptions are. In this way we not only win our client's confidence but also engage his or her conscious mind in verifying our words. Having agreed with the first five parts of our statement, it will agree with the sixth by inertia – i.e. that the individual is indeed breathing steadily – and we thus turn the sixth part into the suggestion we need in this particular case.

An alternative variant of this model might be **A** *or* **A** *or* **A**, *but* **S**, as in:

1) I wonder if you want A
2) to keep your eyes open, A
3) or you want to close them A
4) or simply let them rest, A
5) but I'm sure you'll feel the most appropriate
   moment S
6) for you to relax S

As you have probably guessed, in this case all these words are designed to make our client relax. How exactly do they do that?

Here our client's conscious mind is preoccupied with the dilemma whether to allow the eyes to close or not, and misses the opportunity to resist the suggestion to relax. And then, why resist something that is undoubtedly pleasant for everyone – a good rest? Here is another cue in this sentence!

Yet there is also another one – the expression "I wonder ...", which does not feed the conscious mind any information that requires reasoning, and thus disarms it by depriving it of the opportunity to act and, therefore, to resist.

If you study the sentence carefully, you will find yet another cue – our client's conscious mind might concentrate not on the question of whether he or she *will* relax, but whether he or she *will feel the moment* to relax. The element of doubt is confined to the question *When will it happen?* and not *Will it happen or not?*

And another cue – to close your eyes and to let them rest is sometimes one and the same thing. Perhaps we could also find other cues, because every verbal communication is many-layered.

At any event, in both cases **A** actually paves the way for **S**. Alignment **A** is addressed to the conscious, and suggestion **S** to the subconscious. While the conscious checks the truthfulness of the statements **A**, the subconscious responds directly to the suggestions **S**.

Other models of hypnotic speech could be designed on the same principle. For example, *situation-based* indirect suggestions. Here are several variants:

If **A**, *then* **S**	If you listen to your breathing, you may allow yourself to *relax and prepare for a pleasant trance.*

While **A**, **S**	While listening to my voice, you can *become more and more relaxed.*
A, *while* **S**	You can continue listening to my voice while *your breathing slows and relaxes.*
When **A**, **S**	When the hand touches your knee, *you can close your eyes and relax.*
A, *therefore* **S**	I can see that your body is motionless and your breathing is even, so *you can easily go into a pleasant sleep.*

Needless to say, any **A** may be transformed into **A** *and/or* **A** *and/or* **A** ..., just as any **S** may become **S** *and/or* **S** *and/or* **S** ...

As noted above, an appropriately-phrased communication can disarm the conscious mind or, in other words, take away its dominance. A classic example is: "You *don't know* when your breathing will change and when you'll be ready to relax."

We can also use any already manifested hypnotic phenomena to induce new ones. All that is necessary is to set our suggestion in an acceptable context. For example: "It's wonderful that you have learned how to lose the ability to move. You can now lose the ability to stay awake."

Another way of giving a suggestion is by offering an apparent choice: "You can fall forwards or backwards or sideways." We thus imperceptibly deny our client the options of not falling or of doing something else.

Another effective way of giving indirect suggestions

is by asking questions: "Can you sit in the chair without being able to stand up?" "Could you have forgotten something that occurred during the trance?"

We should pay special attention to suggestions that involve what is known as the *double bind*, via which we offer the client a choice between alternatives that are equally conducive to trance induction. A double bind can be created in several ways. Examples include:

Creating a double bind via a question	"In which direction do you want to sway – *forwards or backwards?*" "Which arm feels *heavier?*" "How do you want to *enter the trance – lying down or sitting?*" etc.
Time-based double bind	"When do you think you can *enter trance – right now or a bit later?*"
Consciously-/unconsciously-oriented double bind	"If your subconscious wants *to go into trance now*, it will move your left hand. If it prefers *to go later*, it will move your right hand."
Dissociatively-oriented double bind	"You can allow *only your body or only your mind* to go to sleep." "You can feel a weight *only in your left arm or only in the rest of your body.*"

The good thing about the double bind is that it allows the client to both give in and win. We thus avoid conscious resistance and conventions.

In fact, the variants of phrasing suggestions are innumerable and depend on the particular circumstances. There is therefore no point in trying to memorise standard formulations. It is more important to keep in mind the principle of phrasing the message – which part of it is addressed to the conscious, and which to the unconscious mind. Once again, the most important thing we should remember is that we should try to use the client's language because that is the most reliable way that our message will be received correctly. We have already determined, after all, that this is the basis of successful hypnotic induction.

Chapter 7
Hypnotic Induction

The essence of hypnotic induction;
Conditions and factors
facilitating hypnosis; Induction techniques

As noted earlier, the hypnotic trance is an altered state of consciousness characterised by the subject's weakened control over cognitive processes. In fact, a trance involves the relinquishing of control over both inner processes and outward behaviour.

What we are looking for when applying hypnosis is a state that allows the client to respond adequately and directly at the subconscious level without any interference from the conscious mind. While conducting this hypnotic process, however, we must recognise something that is of paramount importance. It is that we are not really operating with the true world and events around us but with our *notions and concepts* of them. What we really need to be able to do is to treat an idea or a fact as not necessarily an indisputable truth but as a *notion* of the thing in question; to manipulate universally accepted models of time, space and movement; to play with concepts in a way that helps us turn every suggestion we make into a meaningful and real inner experience of the hypnotised subject. The only way to attain such a state is through communication specifically made up of messages that can deal with the critical faculty of the conscious mind and set direct tasks to the subconscious.

Everything we have said so far is therefore relevant to the question of how to guide someone into hypnosis or how to induce a light, medium or deep trance state in another person. It should be noted that there are both trance induction techniques and what are known as trance deepening techniques of which the main purpose is to attain a more profound trance state. And with reference to this, everything that may be described as a suggestibility test may overlap with a trance deepening technique, thus effectively also being a means of hypnotic induction. Crucially, however, *there is a difference between relaxation and hypnosis.* Relaxation is a physical phenomenon. Hypnosis is a mental phenomenon. Many practitioners claim to apply, or indeed believe that they are applying, hypnosis whereas in fact they are simply inducing physical relaxation in their client – which may be effective too, but does not give access to the client's subconscious. Let us repeat: a person is under hypnosis when we have access to trance phenomena that cannot be induced voluntarily in the normal waking state.

As we have said, hypnotism requires unity and synchrony between the hypnotist and the hypnotised person – both pacing and fulfilling the hypnotic tasks together. This rule does not, however, apply to the authoritarian approach, which requires both creating and emphasising as much as possible the greatest possible distinction between the commander and the commanded, between the person who has full freedom of action and the one who is dependent on the other, between the one who is in full control and the person who is in a trance. It is perhaps precisely because of the emphasis on this distinction that the effect of this type of influence is reduced – it is difficult to win someone's conscious or subconscious cooperation by differentiating yourself from him or her.

With reference to conditions and factors that could facilitate hypnotic trance induction, we should note that they are subjective and unique to each one of us. For example, having established whether the subject is oriented towards the visual, the auditory or the kinesthaetic, we should be able to tell whether the light, temperature or intermittent sounds in the room might distract him or her or conversely help him or her to concentrate. Standardised approaches to basic hypnosis have also come up with standardised methods of hypnotic induction. Going back through the history of hypnosis, we may distinguish several main types of hypnotic induction techniques.

Hypnotic induction techniques that aim to tire the eyes of the hypnotised person – the eye fixation or fixed-gaze methods – are relatively popular. The hypnotised person is usually instructed to fix his or her gaze on a particular object – a light, a hypno-disc, some spot above eye level, or whatever. The hypnotist's mode of speech is then designed to weigh the subject's eyelids down and close the eyes, thus achieving the hypnotic trance.

Quite a few induction methods are based on the principle of progressive relaxation. The hypnotist usually suggests progressive relaxation and the dissipation of tension in different muscular groups in the client's body. The purpose is to induce a trance state via physical relaxation and comfort. Practitioners of such methods, however, should pay special attention to building rapport with the client since, as noted above, the result may be only to achieve simple relaxation rather than hypnosis.

Progressive relaxation techniques may also be combined with appropriate background music intended not only to help the client relax but also potentially to trigger various useful associations.

In the past, what were described as "hypnotic passes" were commonly used by hypnotists. The hypnotist moved his or her hands slowly along the contour of the subject's body at a distance of 3 to 5 centimetres (1 to 2 inches). This was regarded as equalising the body temperatures of them both, causing a feeling of comfortable security and relaxation, so facilitating the onset of the hypnotic trance. Some hypnotists also lit the scene with a blue electric bulb for the purpose.

Another variant of this type of hypnotic induction combines verbal suggestion with light massaging of the temples or crown of the person to be hypnotised. The hypnotist thus not only suggests but also physically induces a sense of comfort and relaxation which facilitates the onset of trance.

Even Charcot in his time discovered that it is possible to induce a hypnotic trance not only in surroundings of physical relaxation and carefully regulated speech but also through sudden and severe shock. In this event the client is usually left for several minutes with eyes closed in full silence in a soundproof room. Then there is a sudden loud gunshot, or the abrupt ring of a deafening bell, or a blinding flash of light, or similar, and the hypnotist commands in a loud and authoritative voice, "Sleep!" This kind of induction has been found to be effective mainly on people of the hysterical type. It is an approach that naturally has many comparable variants, but the key lies foremost in our ability to spot, choose and use exactly the right moment to block the conscious mind by applying the shock, and at that moment give a direct command to the subconscious.

What all these types of induction have in common is that hypnosis is identified with sleep – the main purpose is to "put" the hypnotic subject "to sleep". The important thing, however, is that the physical method by which we guide the subject into hypnosis does not matter provided that there is adequate communication and motivation. Another important thing to remember is that hypnosis is not sleep in the sense of passivity. As we already know, a person under hypnosis has a subconscious choice and can be active – in both outward behaviour and inner experience of various trance phenomena.

While on the topic of how to guide a person into hypnosis, we must also consider how to bring a person out of it. This usually takes much less time than induction. Ending the trance, we must not forget to remove all suggestions of heaviness, drowsiness, fatigue, age regression, etc. Paradoxically, although hypnosis is not always a genuine sleep state, when we bring a person out of trance we are effectively waking him or her up, so that the individual will go through the motions precisely of someone who has just woken up and is reorienting himself or herself in space and time. It would not be unreasonable therefore to approach the issue philosophically once again and predicate that there are different degrees of wakefulness – although to do so would change the original direction of our study of trance.

Before describing in detail a sample technique for inducing a hypnotic trance, we will consider the seven-step hypnotic model applied by Milton Erickson and his followers, since this model contains the major components of hypnotic induction in the most effective sequence:

- *Step 1*: Invite your client to make himself or herself comfortable.
- *Step 2*: Focus his or her attention on some object, task or sensation.
- *Step 3*: Modulate your speech in a way that will dissociate your client's conscious and subconscious mind.
- *Step 4*: Inform your client of all the trance indicators that you observe in him or her as you observe them.
- *Step 5*: Tell your client that there is nothing he or she needs consciously to do.
- *Step 6*: Use the trance and trance phenomena to which you have access for the purpose you have set out to achieve.
- *Step 7*: Bring your client out of the trance.

Clearly, Step 6 involves hypnotherapy – i.e. the use of hypnosis for therapeutic purposes, as discussed in detail in Chapters 8 and 9. As for the other steps in this Ericksonian model, to have mastered them is actually to have mastered the principles of any and every hypnotic induction. This is it in substance, however – the form may vary infinitely. As noted above, hypnosis cannot be a routine procedure because entering and experiencing a trance is unique to every individual. Nevertheless, I intend to present a sample of hypnotic induction which although it cannot serve as a model, can represent a brief reminder of the sequence of the whole process. I will first describe it and then explain it.

My example is that of the induction of a hypnotic trance through hand-shaking.

Have your client sit in a comfortable chair facing you. Take the client's right hand as if you were shaking hands, and try to move it up and down in time with his or her breathing rate until you achieve full synchronisation. Then try to use this hand-shaking to slow and relax the client's breathing, in the rhythm of which you should proceed with your hypnotic speech. You might start like this:

> I will now ask you to take up the position in which you feel most comfortable, in which you feel *comfortable and pleasantly relaxed*, while your breathing becomes *slower and slower, deeper and deeper, and easier and easier.*
>
> I will ask you to close your eyes, to concentrate on your breathing, and I wonder if you will notice the moment at which it will change and become *slow, deep and even*, and ALL THE TENSION IN YOUR BODY WILL start to DIMINISH AND GRADUALLY VANISH ALTOGETHER.

I want you to feel the temperature of the air around you, to feel the touch of your clothes on your skin, to feel the chair beneath you ... to listen to my voice and to regard ANY OTHER SOUND you hear simply as a background to my voice – a background that will FADE OUT AND DISAPPEAR with every breath you take in ... and out ... while you *relax more and more.*

I see that your body is now *passive and still,* and I am sure that YOU ARE LOSING ALL DESIRE TO MAKE ANY MOVEMENT AT ALL, for the slightest movement, the slightest flutter of the eyelids, every time you swallow, every word of mine *is making you feel more and more relaxed and drowsy,* while YOUR BREATHING IS BECOMING EVEN DEEPER, SLOWER AND STEADIER.

You don't have to do anything. ... You don't have to consciously follow the meaning of my words. ... You don't have to move. ... You don't have to stay awake and you don't have to try to SLEEP MORE AND MORE DEEPLY, so you can afford simply to *enjoy this pleasant trance,* this state in which YOUR BODY seems to BE DISAPPEARING, and I wonder which has already fallen asleep – your body or your mind.

Now, *while you are relaxing more and more,* I will start counting slowly from one to ten, and I wonder if you will notice how AT EACH COUNT YOU WILL SLEEP MORE AND MORE DEEPLY, and how AT EACH COUNT YOU WILL COME CLOSER AND CLOSER to a *pleasant state of relaxation and deep and pleasant* SLEEP, because everyone needs a rest.

One ... Two ... Three ...

That's right ... You can afford to relax EVEN MORE with each breath in ... and out, ... in ... and out. ... In a moment I will let go of your right hand and I wonder if it will remain in the air ... and if it will find the most comfortable position in the air ... or if YOU ARE NOW SO RELAXED AND DEEPLY AND PLEASANTLY ASLEEP that your right hand will fall on your knee ...

and when your right hand touches your knee ... you can allow yourself to sleep deeper and deeper still ... while your breathing becomes slower and slower and deeper and deeper.

Four ... Five ... Six ...

That's right ... With every breath in ... and out, ... *deeper and deeper in a pleasant* SLEEP ... in which NOTHING MATTERS EXCEPT MY VOICE. ... And I wonder exactly how DEEP this PLEASANT SLEEP is, into which YOU ARE SINKING MORE AND MORE DEEPLY with every word I say. ...

Seven ... Eight ...

That's right. ... Excellent. ... Because **it's really so nice to simply SLEEP ... and to relax** *more and more deeply.* ... **Everyone needs a rest**. ...

Nine ...

In a moment I will say "ten" ... I wonder if you will notice how at the count of TEN you will relax even further and go into a deep and pleasant sleep, in which YOU WILL HEAR MY VOICE ONLY and NOTHING ELSE MATTERS. ... That's right ...

TEN. SLEEP! ... SLEEP! ... Deeply and peacefully. That's right. Excellent. SLEEP *even more and more deeply.*

At this point, then, if we think our client is already in a trance, we can proceed to test the depth of the trance. For example:

I wonder if you feel HOW HEAVY YOUR RIGHT ARM IS. I know that this WILL BE DIFFICULT FOR YOU, but try to raise your right arm. I know that this WILL TIRE YOU, but you will then rest and sleep *even more deeply.*

If this test shows us that our suggestions have achieved the desired effect, we may proceed with more difficult tasks, which may be set by more direct or indirect commands depending on the depth of the trance state. We may test the client for accessible trance phenomena – anaesthesia, amnesia, positive and negative visual, auditory and tactile hallucinations, age regression, etc. – and use those that would be of benefit in the particular case.

The best way to end a hypnosis session is to let the hypnotised person wake up at his or her own pace, but in practice we seldom have either the opportunity or the time – which is why we apply waking techniques. In principle, waking is much quicker than induction, but we must nevertheless give our client an opportunity to reorient without suffering any discomfort and confusion. We should not hesitate to use posthypnotic suggestion to "sugarcoat" how our client will feel after emerging from hypnosis. We may wake him or her up like this:

> Now I want you to rest well, because I will shortly start counting backwards from ten to one, and AT EACH COUNT YOU WILL WAKE UP MORE AND MORE … AT EACH COUNT YOUR BODY WILL RECOVER ITS TONE AND YOU WILL FEEL MORE AND MORE ALERT AND RESTED. At the count of "one" you will wake up *fresh, alert, rested and in an excellent mood.* But now simply REST some more, and when you open your eyes at the count of "one" this *pleasant feeling of lightness and peace* will remain. … Ten. Nine. Eight. Seven. Six.
>
> Five …
> Four …
> Three …
> Two …
> One.

This, then, is an example of hypnotic induction and posthypnotic waking. Let us examine in greater detail some of the elements of the example in order to explain as fully as possible the full purpose of the expressions and phrases used so carefully by the hypnotist.

We must first note that it is best to align our speech tempo with our client's breathing rate. According to some hypnotists, cues should be given as the subject breathes in. It is believed that the cues are then easier to assimilate – they are, so to speak, taken in as naturally and spontaneously as a breath of air.

Other hypnosis professionals claim conversely that cues should be given as the client breathes out. The logic is that people speak as they exhale, and they thus take in what they are being told under hypnosis as if they themselves are saying it, assimilating it with lowered resistance from the conscious mind.

So far there are no sufficiently reliable facts proving the degree of effectiveness of either of these two theories. The most important thing for us to remember is to develop the habit of aligning our speech tempo with our client's breathing rate. It is after that a matter of personal choice whether to give our cues upon the client's inhalation or the client's exhalation, just as it is a matter of choice whether in inducing the trance we count from one up to a particular number or count backwards down to one.

If you look at the example of induction presented above, you will note that it is printed in several different styles of type (ordinary roman, italics, capitals and bold type). It is difficult to convey all the shades and inflections of intonation that a hypnotist may use during trance induction, but I have done my best to suggest at least a proportion of the modulation by means of these variations in type style.

In addition to elaborating on what style I have intended to refer to each modulation, however, I should like to explain various other factors in the example by going through the whole thing once more step by step.

1   I repeat this because it is important: the hypnotist must speak slowly and in a carefully regulated tone in synchronisation with the client's breathing; he or she must speak in a confident – but not assertive – voice. Then he or she may gradually slow down, thus also slowing down the client's breathing. It is this sort of speech that is referred to by everything printed in ordinary roman type.

2   Phrases like "*...comfortable and pleasantly relaxed...*", "*...slower and slower, deeper and deeper, and easier and easier....*," "*...making you feel more and more relaxed and drowsy...*," and "*...enjoy this pleasant trance...*" actually describe the atmosphere we want to create in the hypnotic process. If we say them in a different tone of voice (e.g. slower, steadier and deeper), the subconscious will notice and distinguish them from the rest of our verbal communications. We can thus implant the requisite soothing and relaxing suggestions in the fertile soil of the subconscious, bypassing the critical faculty of the conscious mind. They are printed in italics.

3   We have defined direct and indirect suggestions in previous chapters. We have also noted that this distinction is a matter of convention only. We may nonetheless say that indirect suggestions are suggestions

that in fact access the subconscious directly – i.e. they slip through the net of the conscious mind and go straight to the subconscious. In the example above, such suggestive phrases are in all capitals. They actually represent a concealed form of direct command, hidden in the flow of speech but to be pronounced in a slightly louder, firmer, more confident and imperative voice. They can thus be distinguished from the rest of the message, becoming a wholly different message. Let us take the following example: "I will ask you to close your eyes, to concentrate on your breathing, and I wonder if you will notice the moment at which it will change and become *slow, deep and even*, and ALL THE TENSION IN YOUR BODY WILL start to DIMINISH AND GRADUALLY VANISH ALTOGETHER." The meaning of all this is that the client is invited to relax and told that all the tension that is in his or her body will disappear. That, at least, is the message the conscious mind receives. But the subconscious identifies and absorbs yet another aspect and message, which is direct –"All the tension in your body will diminish and gradually vanish!" at a continuous and increasing rate – which is marked out only by the change in intonation. This is a very convenient way of making indirect suggestions.

4   As you might have noticed, some phrases in the sample hypnotic induction patter are truisms – i.e. statements that express an undoubted and self-evident truth – as is, for example, the universally valid "Everyone needs a rest." Truisms help us win the confidence of a person we want to hypnotise because he or she cannot but agree with us. Moreover, using such truisms may help clients to develop a habit of agreeing with us, thus lulling the critical faculty of their conscious minds to sleep. This,

in its turn, would help us lead them to a state in which they will agree by inertia – i.e. along with the truisms they will also accept our suggestions as indisputable truth. Which of course is precisely our purpose.

5   You might also find in the technique detailed above some examples of double bind, dissociation, suggestion via a question and other devices outlined in the previous chapter. One such example is: "… and I wonder which has already fallen asleep – your body or your mind." Even this simple half-sentence is an excellent example of many-layered communication in that through it, by itself, we achieve several very important things. First, we ask the question *which* – the body or the mind – has already fallen asleep, thus shifting the conscious mind's doubt onto the question *which* – and not *whether* – something is asleep. Second, with this question we *dissociate* the body from the conscious mind; we dissociate physical from mental phenomena; we give the subject a chance to recognise the dual nature of himself or herself through direct experience. Third, we create a double bind – i.e. we give our client a dual choice, both of the alternatives of which are favourable to us.

6   It is very important that we regulate our speech in a way that is totally disarming – i.e. that strips our client's conscious mind of its dominant role while establishing communication with the subconscious. The following phrase is an example of one way of doing this: "You don't have to consciously follow the meaning of my words …"

In fact, we could find many more implicit cues in the above example of the hypnotist's hypnosis induction speech, and if you study it carefully you will see that not a single word, phrase or punctuation mark is accidental. A detailed interpretation, however, is unnecessary for those who are sufficiently advanced; indeed, it might do a disservice to those who seriously intend to make progress in hypnotism, because no training could replace personal experience and practice.

Naturally, there are many ways of inducing hypnosis. However, the approach described above is an appropriate starting-point because it facilitates alignment with the subject's nonverbal behaviour: let us recall that we are holding the other person's hand and are thus in physical contact with him or her. In this way we can not only control the subject's breathing through our hand-shaking movements but also feel how relaxed and heavy the hand is and thus get a clear idea of the effectiveness of our suggestions.

Some may be surprised at the proposition that it is unnecessary to list or describe in detail a wide variety of induction techniques. Yet if you read this and the previous chapter carefully, you will realise that they present verbal and nonverbal techniques of trance induction in detail that is entirely sufficient. All the individual instruments of this hypnotic orchestra are like multifunctional pieces of a mosaic that may be arranged in countless patterns and pictures. Or, in other words, while I feel free to present just the principles of hypnotism, you will have the inestimable pleasure of discovering for yourself the different forms of hypnotic induction in all their magical variety and flexibility.

Chapter 8
Hypnotherapy

The history and evolution of hypnotherapy;
Schools and approaches in psychotherapy;
Traditional and Ericksonian hypnotherapy

Before we take a close look at hypnotherapy, I ought
to say a few words about psychotherapy in general. As the
term itself suggests in its etymology, the psychotherapist's
task is to heal the "spirit", just as the physician's task is
to care for the patient's bodily health. Talking of health,
however, we should consider the question whether there
is such a thing as " the completion of therapy". We might
say that a person is healthy if he or she is not suffering
from any diseases or disorders that affect the normal vital
functions. But is that enough? After all, a Tibetan yogi
who dries a wet sheet with his body heat up in the Hima-
layan mountains at a temperature of –40 degrees Celsius
is surely much healthier than that. One can simply always

be healthier – i.e. better suited for life in both physical and mental terms (some call this an aspiration for perfection) – and in this sense therapy need never be complete. Therapy simply continues without a therapist. To make the mistake of denying this line of thinking is also rather unwisely to refute the fact that prevention is better than cure – yet we all know that it is much easier to prevent something than to cure it. As an old saying goes, the best woodcutter in the woods is he who cuts the trees that have already fallen.

So let us now concentrate on psychotherapy. There are many kinds of psychotherapeutic treatment – Freud's orthodox psychoanalysis and the successive psychodynamic schools, cognitive-behavioural and behavioural-cognitive psychotherapy, Fritz Perls' Gestalt therapy, Virginia Satir's family therapy, Jacob Moreno's psychodrama, Victor Frankl's logotherapy, Stanislaw Grof's holotropic therapy, art and music therapy, group psychotherapy, hypnotherapy, short-term strategic therapy. (To avoid professional snobbery, we ought to add to this list all the primitive and archaic forms of psychotherapy such as "casting the bones" against fear, chanting occult spells, etc.) Patients with identical symptoms may undergo any one of the above-mentioned therapies and their conditions will improve (or not) to an equal (or different) extent, but by different means. An extensive survey of the outcome of the various psychotherapeutic methods has found that they are all as effective as each other. Accordingly, it is very difficult to identify the limits of psychotherapy, because any potential patient may be influenced and the whole of his or her life might be changed drastically by trivial and, at face value, fortuitous events – by reading a particular book, by seeing a particular film, by hearing a particular phrase or even by reading a particular word, by a dream's coming true, by taking an ordinary walk up a hill in the suburbs, etc.

It is hard to define and put parameters to the term "psychotherapy". What we do know, however, is that if we go back in time we will discover the roots of psychotherapy as far back as at the dawn of human civilisation. But there is no point in going back to Chapter 1 of this book and reviewing the birth of hypnosis and the pioneers of hypnotherapy. Instead, we will examine the main differences between the two main schools of psychotherapy – by convention divided between the long-term and the short-term (including hypnotherapy) approaches.

Long-term psychotherapeutic approaches, then, are based on the principles of Freudian psychoanalysis. Generally, the main task is to identify the cause of the patient's symptoms. The logic is that by removing the cause via cathartic re-experience and recognition of the situation that caused the trauma, we also remove the symptoms resulting from the trauma. In this line of thought, the main question asked by psychoanalysis and the other long-term therapeutic approaches is *why* the patient is as he or she is today – i.e. what is the *reason* for the condition? The therapist therefore concentrates on determining the cause rather than on treating the particular symptoms.

On the other hand, short-term psychotherapeutic approaches focus on the symptoms. The therapist's attention and efforts centre on the fastest (and safest) way possible to eliminate physical and/or mental distress – anxiety, depression, addiction, headache, or whatever. The main question for short-term therapy practitioners is *how* their client can be helped to cope with the *particular symptom*. The focus is not on the past but on the future.

Long-term psychotherapy claims that short-term psychotherapy ignores the crucial thing – the cause of distress, which is encapsulated somewhere in the subconscious and will simply replace one dire symptom with another unless and until it is discovered.

Short-term therapy claims that what is most important is not the cause – of which we can at best be only 99 per cent sure when we find it that it is really what we have been looking for – and that long-term therapy has a one-sided view of the subconscious, seeing only its negative effects and disregarding its positive potential.

- Long-term therapy told short-term therapy that it was too young and immature.
- Short-term therapy responded by saying that long-term therapy smelled of mothballs.
- Long-term therapy turned away and said it had more important concerns.
- Short-term therapy said that long-term therapy had no idea of what was important and what was not, because it was arrogant enough to insist on taking up a disproportionate amount of people's time on Earth when it had no real need to.
- Long-term therapy claimed that it was right.
- So did short-term therapy.

Hypnotherapy claims that *trance is therapeutic in itself* and that trance states are an invariable part of any psychotherapeutic process – whether short-term or long-term. After all, there have been millennia of human history during which to spend a night in a certain location (a temple, particularly, but otherwise a cave, among ruins, or somewhere out in the mountains) was assumed to predispose some sort of healing power.

In fact, each individual psychotherapeutic approach is more effective for an individual group of specific problems. Hypnotherapy is not a panacea either, and it is appropriate most of all for afflictions associated with clear and distinct symptoms – phobias, addictions, bad habits, etc. It is an entirely different matter that in the early 1970s hypnotherapy split into "traditional" and "non-traditional". As we have seen, that was primarily due to Milton H. Erickson, who turned the idea of psychotherapy upside down, proved the effectiveness of his therapeutic methods, and won recognition as a greater contributor to the practice of psychotherapy than Freud had been to the theory of psychotherapy. This is no longer a matter of dispute because there are too many facts in the case that speak for themselves.

As regards traditional techniques in hypnotherapy, it must be noted that they are based on the authoritarian approach in hypnotism, which uses direct suggestions and commands designed specifically to "programme" the client's behaviour. Of course such approaches have their place in psychotherapy (Milton Erickson himself mastered them to perfection and did not hesitate to apply them whenever he judged necessary), but what limits their effectiveness and their use is that the client must be in a very deep trance for those direct programming suggestions to be accepted uncritically by his or her subconscious.

The other problem is the responsibility as hypnotherapist for knowing precisely what to suggest – because, as noted above, every verbal suggestion given in trance is interpreted entirely literally and unambiguously. Since we all use words in a different way, it must indisputably be more sensible to avoid any risk of misunderstanding, especially when what is at stake is the mental health and well-being of someone who has allowed us into the least-known realm of his or her person. I believe we would all agree that to reduce hypnotherapeutic trance to simply giving orders to the client about his or her behaviour suggests a methodology that is somewhat humiliating to the client, and which tends to distort the concept of hypnotism and therapy in general. The false assumption here is that hypnotherapy is supposed to give clients something they do not have – courage, peace of mind, confidence, will-power, etc. This is a rather pretentious proposition, which is to some degree incompatible not only with the therapeutic perception but also with the perceptions of anyone who claims to have some knowledge of human nature. It would be much more reasonable to assume that we neither know nor could possibly learn in full every single aspect of every individual's unique being – which means that we have no right to place their mental health at risk by treating them as though something that was valid for an individual with an identical symptom was bound to be valid for them too.

Rather than go on immediately to launch into a digression in order to review and critique some dated concepts in the "traditional" approaches in hypnotherapy, I will take a short cut and say a few words about the cases in which direct suggestion can be used effectively in healing the "spirit".

One of the main methods of hypnotherapy is based on the psychoanalytical concept of psychic determinism, according to which all mental suffering (and all behaviour generally) is rooted in past trauma, usually during childhood. If we imagine the structure of the mind, we may visualise the subconscious as the part of the iceberg that lies underwater (according to Freud's famous metaphor), whereas the conscious is the relatively tiny tip above the surface (see *Figure 5*).

Figure 5

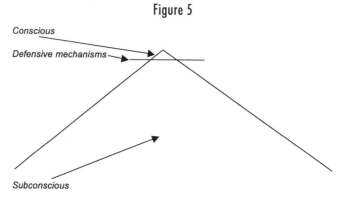

If we assume that any specific situation is not traumatic in itself – it is the attitude or reaction to this particular situation that is traumatic – we may conclude that every person has experienced suffering in a multitude of forms. Some of those traumas – as they are by convention called – would cause constant emotional distress if we were continuously aware of them, so the subconscious has "wrapped them up" and limited their access to the conscious mind by means of various defensive mechanisms.

Although those traumatic complexes do not have direct access to the surface of the conscious mind, they exercise a tangible influence on the entire dynamic of the subconscious, and thus on modes of behaviour. The therapeutic logic in psychoanalysis is to break down or bypass the defensive mechanisms that protect the conscious from the attacks of the subconscious. In other words, the situation that has most probably caused the symptom must be identified and relived so as to enable a change in the client's attitude to that particular situation – which will actually change his or her entire psychodynamic.

More or less the same result can also be achieved through hypnosis (the method has even been called hypnoanalysis), and without any need to overcome defensive mechanisms – because if the conscious mind is then (figuratively speaking) absent, so are the defensive mechanisms, which have nothing to protect from the unpleasant aspect of the subconscious.

In fact, according to the logic of psychic determinism, the crucial thing is to pinpoint the situation that has caused the specific trauma – psychoanalysis and hypnosis simply do it in different ways.

If we follow this logic and apply hypnosis, we should not assume that our client has necessarily to be in a very deep trance because, as noted above, the important thing is to gain direct access to his or her subconscious. It should be enough to identify the trauma and make the client relive it under the influence of our suggestions and comments, which would change the client's attitude to the event in question and thus help him or her overcome its negative effects.

Another case in which we could readily resort to direct suggestions is when we want to use hypnotic trance for pain relief – as fairly often applied in general medical practice and in dentistry. We have all surely heard or read about surgery, childbirth and dental extraction under hypnosis without anaesthetics. At the beginning of the twenty-first century this comes as no big news to anybody. In such cases we simply need at least a medium – preferably a deep – trance state, in which we directly suggest to the patient that a particular part of his or her body is numb or less sensitive or dissociated from the rest of the body.

Incidentally, if as you are reading this you think that what I am saying about the approaches in hypnotism ordinarily regarded as traditional seems facile, let me assure you that I am not oversimplifying, but the fact is that these methods have reached their sell-by date. "Traditional" hypnosis has had its youth as well as its heyday, and it has also fulfilled a noble yet ticklish mission – namely, to rehabilitate trance in therapy and science. However, instead of abiding by the natural law of ascent and decline, hypnosis – with its inherent mystique – reached a peak and then started over, experiencing a renaissance and evolving into something that is even more effective, more advanced and closer to life and people. The most amazing thing about that is that this revitalising transformation, this whole new lease of life, is the result of the personal effort, example and philosophy of a crusader who has blazed the trail for a multiplicity of further innovations and an army of followers. We must give the credit to Milton H. Erickson – master of hypnosis, creator of short-term strategic therapy, teacher of a whole generation of brilliant therapists and researchers, inspirer of new quests and, above all, a striking example of the power of the human spirit. In other words, a great ordinary man.

Examining Milton Erickson's practices and therapeutic principles in detail, we discover, along with his rich and varied techniques, a hidden, timely and competent paradoxical methodology of inaction, which was sufficiently effective to be of invaluable help in the solution of cases while at the same time being so simple and inconspicuous that clients discovered that they were their own best therapists.

In considering the essence of the Ericksonian approach to hypnotherapy, we must keep in mind that it is extremely difficult to identify and study all aspects of Erickson's therapeutic practices and to categorise his knowledge and skills in this field. This is because of his extraordinary creativity, his almost childlike curiosity about the world and people, as well as his incredible powers of observation and perspicacity, which more than made up for his physical handicaps and poor health. All the more so in that Erickson was not concerned with theorising about his therapeutic approaches. He published only the odd paper here and there himself, so that in fact the most important aspects and even some of the basics of his methods were studied in detail, perfected and described by his students and disciples: Jay Haley, Ernest Rossi, Jeffrey Zeig, John Grinder and Richard Bandler, Steven Gilligan, Jean Beccio and others. On the other hand, it is not really accurate now to say that any particular hypnotist is specifically a devotee of Milton Erickson – for the simple reason that to practise Ericksonian hypnosis and therapy you must not only rely on your own knowledge but you must also have access to the inexhaustible sources of *your own* personal uniqueness and inner self-knowledge. And yet, in endeavouring to present Milton Erickson's ideas and practices in a coherent way, we must note from the very beginning his therapeutic motto, which runs like a fine golden thread through each aspect not only of his work, but also of his philosophy in life: *Experience is our only teacher*! And since we have already said quite a few things about the trance state, about communication between the left and right hemispheres of the brain, about hypnotic induction and hypnotic phenomena, we can now move on to some of the basic principles of Ericksonian hypnotherapy.

I am perfectly aware that I am incapable of explaining the philosophy of Ericksonian therapy better than the founders of that theoretical-and-practical movement, so I will turn to "the real thing", leaving Milton Erickson's words to fulfil their original purpose and speak for themselves.

The first major objective of Ericksonian short-term strategic hypnotherapy is thus to have therapist and client concentrate their efforts on *realistic goals*. Otherwise, of course, the entire therapeutic process is doomed to failure. It is neither feasible nor moral or professional to promise your client eternal happiness (even figuratively). Although it might be entirely well-intended, such an ambition could lead to numerous wrong conceptions and expectations and subsequently to a number of complications. As Milton H. Erickson puts it, the task of psychotherapy is to help a patient achieve, as successfully as possible, the goal he or she is aiming at.

That is it exactly. No ambition on the psychotherapist's part for total control over the details let alone the larger aspects of the client's life – a temptation that has caused more than one psychotherapist to stray.

I would like to point up another Ericksonian statement that I believe is especially important: "I am firmly against any ambition to achieve perfection, an ambition pursued by some doctors and psychologists in their work with people," says Erickson; and he continues: "I have never met a perfect human being and I don't believe I ever will. I believe it is precisely that imperfection which you are trying to take away from a person that makes him [or her] fascinating and enables you to distinguish this individual from others and remember him [or her]."

This is a principle fundamental to Erickson's therapeutic philosophy, and one that has been adopted by his disciples too. A wonderful example of a positive outlook on human nature, in stark contrast to the traditional psychotherapeutic view which usually points an accusing finger at different aspects of our being.

Another main task of Ericksonian hypnotherapy is to *focus the therapeutic process squarely on the future rather than on the past.* This is one of the main differences between the Ericksonian and psychodynamic-oriented therapeutic approaches.

According to Erickson, insights into the past might prove useful in terms of general awareness, but those insights cannot change the past. If in the past you were jealous of your mother, this has already become a factor in your life. If you were obsessed with or even fixated on your mother, this has also become a factor in your life.

You may be able to obtain all kinds of insights into your past, but even if you do, you can no longer change it. Yet the patient lives in the here and now, having to deal with what is happening today. That is why the course of psychotherapy should be oriented towards the fact that the patient is living today and will be thinking of life tomorrow and what the next week and the next year has in store for him or her.

As noted above, Erickson thought that only *immediate experience could lead to change*. He also believed that specific behavioural activity recommended by the therapist could evoke the required therapeutic experience, and that was the purpose of one of his favourite techniques: setting therapeutic assignments. Erickson recommended bringing the patient to the point at which he or she would be amazed to discover his or her own potential in action, which is much more effective than sitting back and passively observing what the therapist has been doing with them.

Unlike the theory and practice of psychoanalysis – which talks of resistance by the patient in a way that largely relieves the therapist of responsibility for the treatment – the Ericksonian approach is the very opposite. Any resistance from the client is due to the client's symptoms, and the client is not to blame for them. Responsibility for the treatment is thus assumed almost entirely by the therapist – provided, however, that there is maximum commitment (according to the client's abilities) to the therapeutic process on the part of the client. It is the therapist who is obliged to create the appropriate atmosphere, to determine the precise means and mode of motivation, to win the client's confidence and cooperation, to accept the client's limitations and to decode the received information. The therapist must also *recognize the reality of the client's problem* and provide protection and support, while at the same time giving the client the freedom required for the natural and undeviating progress of the therapeutic process. Despite all this responsibility, the main figure in therapy is the client, and everything is done in the name of his or her well-being. After all, therapy is possible without a therapist, but certainly not without a client. In this respect, Erickson notes something very important: sometimes when patients come to you for help they might resist your help – but at the same time they will be desperately hoping you will overcome that resistance.

One other thing that distinguishes the Ericksonian approach from most psychotherapeutic practices is its *prima facie* casual, improvised and informal character. Milton Erickson was an outspoken opponent of what was considered classic therapeutic behaviour. What he wanted and encouraged his students to achieve was to dispel such fossilised notions of this kind of behaviour – to shed the shackles of canons outlining the limits of professionalism in psychotherapy – because what is crucial to achieving our goals, therapeutic or otherwise, is retaining our freedom of action. We must be able to create and maintain as many alternatives as possible, helping us to stick to the course we have chosen. If we choose to remain within the confines of a particular model of behaviour defined as "professionalism", we allow ourselves far less room for manoeuvre than our clients, whose problems usually give them the right to be fluid and unpredictable. Yet if we consider the quotation above (about client resistance), we will realise that neither they nor we stand to gain in any way from a possible victory on the part of the client. In sum, aligning oneself with the notion of what a professional should be like does not necessarily mean that you *are* a professional. To quote Erickson again: "I do not aim to be a professional cultivating in himself [or herself] a sense of self-dignity. I simply do things which make the patient act in a way that is right and beneficial for him [or her]. Because it is not a matter of professional dignity, but of professional competence."

And again: "The psychotherapist's consulting room is simply a place where two human beings meet for the purpose of solving a concrete problem. You must be first and foremost a human being and you must drop your professional tone and manners, so that patients can trust precisely the human in you."

In fact this informal, unconventional, and sometimes distinctly odd model of behaviour may justifiably be defined as strategic, because it allows us to use surprise as a weapon in the therapeutic process which is very much like a duel – a duel in which the therapist is on the client's side.

One of the main attributes in the arsenal of Ericksonian hypnotherapy is *humour*. This is of paramount importance, because humour removes any aspect of criticality, dispels anxiety and helps the client cope with distress that he or she has no intrinsic need to experience. Humour helps a client find comfort in distress, or at least find an alternative mode of being that is favourable to them. In fact, many case studies of the work of Milton Erickson are specifically related as anecdotes, for he had a wonderful sense of humour and used it extensively in his work. To laugh while you work, create, learn, treat others and yourself, is not only fun but also a supreme achievement. Surely everybody would agree that it would be silly to throw away such life-giving water from our flasks – especially when we can offer it to a client who has roamed the desert of despair for years. And that is precisely where the majority of people who come knocking on the psychotherapist's door come from.

I must admit that it has been very hard for me to resist the temptation of recounting some of Erickson's most interesting cases ... but I do not want to risk doing an injustice to his theoretical and practical legacy by presenting it as if from one aspect only and thus creating a false impression.

With reference to Ericksonian hypnosis and therapeutic methods, we can say that no single style of psychotherapy exists in a "pure" form. Every approach is eclectic to a greater or lesser degree. The main difference between the Ericksonian and the others, however, lies in the understanding that the client knows much more than the therapist not only about his or her problem but also about the way in which he or she can deal with it. Of course, this is associated with the huge and unmeasured positive potential of our subconscious. Erickson would often tell his patients: "I don't need to know your problem in order to help you solve it."

Now, that is a truly weird thing to say. Yet what is even stranger is that almost always it proved to be true.

We all know that balance in nature requires that every

thing must contain its opposite within itself. It is a commonplace that problems carry their own solutions. In therapy, therefore, the solution lies where the problem is – in the client. And the person that has a better chance of finding this solution is thus not the therapist but the client, because he or she rediscovers things about himself or herself and acquires the necessary knowledge by intensively re-experiencing all his or her disappointments, discoveries, sufferings, joys, desires and, last but not least, positive or negative experience, which brings him or her one step closer to the end of the journey he or she has undertaken in an effort to achieve the desired change. The therapist's duty is to provide the initial impetus that is required for achieving the desired therapeutic goals.

Milton Erickson came up with a brilliant metaphor that explains the main principle in psychotherapy very clearly.

Psychotherapy, he said, is similar to the domino effect – you push the first domino and all the others fall in succession. All you need to do in psychotherapy is to ensure that just the one thing that needs correcting in the patient's behaviour is corrected. If you do that, all other changes will occur naturally.

I will take this opportunity to add yet another distinctive feature of the Ericksonian approach to the list: the use of metaphorical tales and stories ("teaching tales", as Erickson called them) associated with the client's problem. With the help of this technique we can suggest one or several favourable alternatives to our client; we can communicate things that might arouse resistance if told directly, or we can simply test the waters, observing the client's reactions and associations triggered by our story.

I do not delude myself that this overview can cover all aspects of Ericksonian hypnotherapy – a subject discussed in hundreds of books – so I will repeat that the most important thing in Erickson's methods is practice, or the translation of theory and philosophy into action. I will end this theoretical exposition by reiterating that we do not have two schools in hypnotherapy for the simple reason that Ericksonian hypnosis is a natural evolutionary advance and improvement on the hypnotic techniques and methods that were familiar before Milton H. Erickson.

At this point we must also mention neuro-linguistic programming (NLP), created in the early 1970s by mathematician Richard Bandler and linguist John Grinder, both students of Milton Erickson. Their original purpose was to study the cognitive and behavioural patterns of people who in their professional lives had shown the highest level of effectiveness in the spheres of therapy, learning and business. Bandler and Grinder therefore compiled a step-by-step study and analysis of these people's roads to success.

The term "neuro-linguistic programming" might sound daunting but logically and etymologically it is quite accurate. *Neuro*, because it concerns neurology in the form of the neurons or nerve cells of the brain through which we perceive reality. *Linguistic* because it refers to language as the system of communication that encodes the way in which we experience the self, life, the universe and everything. And *programming* implies, figuratively, the imposition of a programme or plan.

In other words, we are talking about software for the brain.

You may think that this makes the whole thing sound too mechanical (or, as industrial psychologists would say, mechanistic). With its undoubtedly useful instruments, NLP is a very effective method of improving various aspects of our functioning lives. The creators of NLP themselves, Grinder and Bandler, described their work as "modelling" behaviour and inner states, and compared it to the putting together of culinary recipes that might make a good cook out of anyone who followed them. It sounds pretentious, but it is hardly accidental that the popularity of and demand for NLP have been growing by leaps and bounds across the civilised world.

To avoid changing the subject from hypnosis to NLP, we will note only the major principles in the philosophy of this contemporary school of attaining self-realisation.

1   There is no such thing as ineffective experience. There is only experience, which tells us whether we have been effective, or not.
2   Individuals have all the resources they need. What they need is timely access to them.
3   Everything achievable may be achieved by anyone provided that there is a maximally detailed algorithm for the purpose.

In the chapter on hypnotic communication we examined NLP's three types of sensory perception systems, so we will not return to the subject. We will note only that NLP is not simply a theory or system of beliefs: NLP is a modern psychological mechanism for studying and acquiring a better understanding of human nature and its hidden potential. I would only add that NLP is still at the dawn of its development, and we are yet to see its zenith.

Let us repeat that we owe this gift of human knowledge to Milton H. Erickson too, and end this chapter with a quote from one of the luminaries of traditional hypnosis, the outstanding scholar Andre Weitzenhoffer. Weitzenhoffer, who knew Erickson personally, described him as

> The greatest master of verbal and nonverbal communication, ... who lives up to his byname Mister Hypnosis ... above all a therapist whose arsenal and knowledge in clinical hypnosis transcend the normal boundaries.

This assessment of Erickson and his legacy is invaluable because it comes from an ideological opponent in a paper in which Weitzenhoffer recounts, among other things, how he himself was hypnotised by Erickson without even realising it.

Chapter 9
The Therapeutic Use of Hypnotic Techniques and Phenomena in Psychotherapy

The principles of hypnotherapy;
Methods and approaches; Some interesting cases

With hypnosis there is one essential thing to note from the very beginning, and that is that a mastery of hypnotism is not a sufficient reason or qualification for its therapeutic use. This does not mean that hypnosis hides mysterious dangers, but that a casual attitude combined with ignorance and a consequent excess of self-confidence could certainly produce deleterious results and do serious harm. Ordinarily, however, things never reach that stage. Just as in any other field of human activity, you must simply know what you are doing.

In thinking about practising hypnotherapy, we should bear in mind that, as we have seen, no psychotherapeutic method exists in pure form. In hypnotherapy too, cases in which the client must be put under hypnosis in almost every therapeutic session are very rare. Normally, in each therapeutic case there is just one or maybe a couple of moments in which a trance state would be of tremendous benefit. We should not forget, however, that *the effectiveness of suggestion does not depend on the depth of the hypnotic trance* – i.e. suggestions given in the waking state may be just as effective as those made in hypnotic trance. The only difference arises from the way in which the suggestions are given.

As noted above, hypnotherapy is not a panacea: it is primarily an appropriate method of treating bad habits and addictions such as smoking, alcoholism, some cases of drug addiction and nutritional disorders. It is also effective in curing various phobias, manias, depressions, and so forth.

Another frequently asked question concerns regressive hypnosis, by which people most often mean a "return" to "past lives". It must be noted here that we are actually working with the client's own spiritual beliefs. It is not for us to give a definitive answer to one of the great philosophical questions, "What happens after death?" But we can certainly say that if our client believes in reincarnation and if his or her spiritual beliefs can help him or her to deal with the current problems, it would be unpardonable to neglect regressive hypnosis even if our own spiritual beliefs do not necessarily coincide with those of the person who has turned to us for help.

The guiding notion in our psychotherapeutic work should be the fact that we must have more freedom, ideas and alternatives for action than our client, and necessarily fewer prejudices and limitations – at least as regards the client's particular complaint. Otherwise, there is no way at all that we can be effective – because we would then be suffering the same problem as the client.

We must recognise the fact that almost all psychological problems are actually problems of communication (communication not only with others but also with one's self). That is why it is words that are the psychotherapist's "scalpel", the "operation" consisting therefore of precise and purposeful communication designed to help the client find more alternatives while rediscovering his or her innate ways of dealing with problem situations.

More specifically, there are techniques that can be applied, designed precisely for trance-based therapy. One of the techniques widely applied by Milton H. Erickson and developed extensively by the creators of NLP, John Grinder and Richard Bandler, is what is known as *anchoring*. Grinder and Bandler define anchoring thus:

> Anchoring is in many ways a practical variant of the stimulus-response model in behaviourism. Still, there are several important differences between the two, namely:
>
> 1 "Establishing a trigger or anchor" does not require an extensive period of time in order to create an identifiable stimulus that triggers the respective response.
> 2 Establishing a connection between anchor and response does not require any additional encouragement. That is, the anchor is established without any immediate reward whatsoever. A reward

or encouragement would facilitate anchoring, but they are not a *conditio sine qua non*.

3   Inner experience (cognitive behaviour) is just as important as behaviourally measurable responses. In other words, NLP holds that the inner dialogue, picture or sensation are in themselves a response that is identical to salivation in the case of Pavlov's dog.

In fact, things are not as confusing as they might seem on first reading this. If we think about it we should realise that we commonly associate a particular inner state with a specific external stimulus. For example, someone may say, "Whenever I hear an ambulance siren, my stomach churns and I start worrying." In this case the wail of the ambulance siren is the stimulus – the anchor – which triggers the respective response. One other thing we could say in this particular case is that this particular association between stimulus and response might have been caused by a *single* actual – probably unpleasant – experience, which, however, was strong enough to create a stable behavioural and cognitive model. We can all identify such anchors that determine not only our behaviour but also the way we feel in particular situations.

The technique of establishing such an anchor is widely used in hypnotherapy and especially in NLP. It is very simple and yet very effective. Let us consider a hypothetical case.

We have a client who complains of panic attacks (he is anxious and nervous, and his mind goes blank) whenever he has to sit for an exam or an interview, and this impacts severely on his performance.

One of the possible approaches is to use trance induction. We could put this client into a trance and use age regression to discover a situation in which he felt calm, self-confident and in full control. What we are concerned most about is not the situation itself but the specific sensation and experience. We can then instruct our client under hypnosis to experience this sense of confidence and self-assurance. While our client is experiencing the concrete positive sensation, we could ask him to, say, clasp his hands together. This handclasp, which should last at least 15 or 20 seconds, then becomes the anchor or trigger "fixed" to the specific inner state.

We could then proceed to use other trance phenomena – for example, future projection. We help our client under hypnosis to mentally project himself into a situation that would cause him to be anxious and nervous. At the same time we make him use the anchor – the handclasp – to trigger the previous sensation of self-confidence and self-assurance.

Thereafter we may help our client develop the habit of feeling the way he wants whenever he wants to. Our goal should not be for him to form a habit of clasping his hands whenever he is in a potentially distressing situation. Our goal should be to turn every situation of this kind into an anchor triggering the sensation of calmness and self-confidence.

Needless to say, this is only an outline presentation of a possible case. The result invariably depends on the appropriate application of every therapeutic technique – i.e. on the extent to which therapeutic communication is used properly, and therefore effectively, throughout the therapeutic process.

Using anchors is especially popular in treating bad habits and addictions, "bad habits" meaning any uncontrolled, unhealthy and recurrent behaviour such as smoking, alcoholism and nutritional disorders. Such behaviour is, after all, usually a response triggered by a particular stimulus.

As we know, in general every symptom has a particular task and serves a particular need. In the same way, every behaviour serves a respective need, and this applies especially to bad habits. Three American hypnotherapists – Mark King, William Cohen and Charles Citrenbaum, concerned particularly with the treatment of bad habits – have proposed quite an accurate and clear classification of the most common causes of self-destructive behaviour.

The most common bad habits are smoking, alcoholism and overeating. According to King, Cohen and Citrenbaum, these self-destructive models of behaviour may arise for many different reasons.

For example, smoking might help some people cope with stress. Others might see smoking as a way of self-assertion or, more precisely, of demonstrating their independence or disagreement with popular opinion. Still others might consider cigarettes a form of companionship. And there are those who regard smoking as a pleasure in life and a luxury gift they can give themselves, or who see smoking as a way of imitating their idol, of losing weight, of gaining acceptance in a particular social group or simply of satisfying their craving for nicotine.

With minor differences, the same reasons are also at the core of alcoholism and overeating. We might merely add that alcoholism is all too often an excuse for irresponsible behaviour, and that overindulgence in food is a pretty successful way to avoid intimate relationships which, for one reason or another, the particular individual finds intimidating.

We should keep in mind, however, that the authors of this theory are American and based their study on specific features of the US socio-psychological model. All the same, things are not too different in Europe either. What is important in this case is that those problems may be influenced effectively by hypnotherapy and that using anchors is one of the successful methods by which they may be treated and resolved.

And so, before endeavouring to tackle any particular symptom we must first discover the need it serves.

As one of the therapeutic forms of treatment, we may replace *destructive* with *constructive behaviour*. For example, we may find a more acceptable way of dealing with boredom than smoking, drinking or eating.

Another treatment would be *reframing* – i.e. reformulating or changing the context of the particular purpose or need. For instance, a negative attitude (intimidation due to inexperience or general lack of self-confidence) to sexual relations may be reframed (i.e. redefined, recontextualised, shown in an entirely different light) as a positive one. This would eliminate the need that requires the established destructive behaviour and help the client cope with the respective bad habit.

In this connection, we must also note that the technique of reframing which, as mentioned above, involves reformulating or changing the context of a problem situation, can in fact involve changing the client's attitude to a traumatic experience and, therefore, the client's entire notion of self. Here is a case example of the reframing technique.

Maria [not her real name], 30, suffered from hypochondria, agoraphobia (she had not gone out by herself for three years) and almost constant depression. This progressively deteriorating condition had started six years after the death of her twin sister.

During her first three therapeutic sessions with me Maria spoke mainly about her health problems. When the conversation turned to significant factors and events in her life, she did her best to avoid the subject of her sister's death – people normally try to avoid pain and opening old wounds, so we look for the trauma in those things the client is reluctant to discuss.

We have all had good times and bad times. Maria, however, was behaving as if she had never been happy in her whole life.

At the end of our fourth session I decided to hypnotise her. She entered a deep trance very easily and quickly.

As noted above, Maria had not gone out by herself for three years. She was driven to the sessions by car by one of her relatives, who usually walked her to the door of my room. Leaving her house on her own even for a minute was inconceivable to her.

I gave Maria a direct posthypnotic suggestion, instructing her to go home by herself after the session – her house was about an hour's walk away – and to feel entirely calm along the way. I expressly reminded her to take note of the air, the sky and the smell of trees during her walk. It was a fresh and wonderful afternoon in spring. The acacias were in bloom and there was a pleasant breeze. Without setting her any other tasks, I brought Maria out of trance.

She felt fresh and light-hearted – as I had suggested – and said she wanted to go home alone. I asked her to give me a call when she was back.

About an hour later she called and started telling me enthusiastically how wonderful it had been to simply go for a walk, feel the fragrance of the acacias, the fresh air, the sense of freedom, etc. However, the most important thing she said was, "I'd forgotten that all this was possible!" This meant that she had recalled the existence of the other side of her life too.

I warned her carefully that this wonderful feeling would go away after a couple of hours and that things would take a turn for the worse before actually improving.

And indeed, at the next session Maria complained that she had felt awful all week because after the positive effect of my suggestion had worn off, she had been haunted by all kinds of things from the past she had not thought about for ages. She was reluctant to discuss anything and was in utter despair over any possible improvement in her condition.

I asked her to tell me about her sister. She unconsciously tried to avoid this line of conversation and changed the subject abruptly. I asked her again and her response was the same. For some time both of us – she unconsciously, and I deliberately – tried to impose our respective subjects of conservation on each other. As tension mounted, Maria suddenly fell into a spontaneous trance and started talking to herself rather than to me.

I moved out of her field of vision while she continued staring straight ahead, pouring out her heart. This was a classically cathartic experience. Maria gave a detailed account of her emotional life. I will describe only matters relevant to our subject.

We all know of the strong bond between twins. Maria and her sister were no exception in this respect. What made them different was that while Maria had always been in excellent health, her sister had been constantly plagued by illness. This made Maria feel guilty not only about being healthy but also about being incapable of helping her sister in any way. Her only comfort was a subconscious identification with her sister with the evident intention of sharing her suffering.

Maria's emotional position when her sister died was, "My sister and I are one. Now that her life is over, so is mine." This attitude was enough to explain her subsequent unconsciously self-destructive behaviour – withdrawal from the world of the living via the typical agoraphobic symptoms, an effort to atone for her guilt about her sister by illness and constant suffering. In other words, Maria was effectively punishing herself. However, it was very difficult for her to do so without deluding herself that she really was ill – and that was precisely what she could not keep on doing now that things had become clear to her.

I need hardly describe the intensity and emotional overtones that surfaced during this session. We discussed everything that had happened at our next session. The important thing is that the thought that she had been suffering from an actual medical condition had never crossed her mind. What mattered to her was everything she had remembered and relived.

At this point we can say something more about the role of reframing or reformulating the client's attitude to the traumatic situation.

As noted above, Maria's emotional background line on the situation was, "My sister and I are one. Now that her life is over, so is mine." The last three of the seven therapeutic sessions that she underwent overall helped her reframe the situation: "My sister and I are one. *My life goes on, and so does hers.*" The important part of the reframed context is, of course, the resolution that *my life goes on.* Maria accepted this position – her self-imposed punishment no longer meant what it had meant to her over the previous six years.

At our eighth session she told me that she had booked a 20-day package holiday. I encouraged her, and she went on holiday after a six-year stint of near-solitary confinement.

When she came back, we met several more times and our sessions were pleasant and interesting, their main purpose being to plan her future and help her pick up the threads of her former life.

Maria's therapy continued, but this time as self-therapy – and she was obviously good at it, because she has since started a small family business and for four years now has shown every sign of enjoying life.

Of course, this is only a necessarily brief account of the therapeutic process and of the whole story, and it is intended simply as an example of the use of hypnosis and the value of reframing.

While we are on the subject of specific techniques in hypnotherapy, we must also mention the *polar* methods devised by Ernest Rossi. These methods are based on the concept of the dual nature of the micro- and macrocosm. Examining this concept from the perspective of human nature, we may assume that every feeling and sensation has only one single polar equivalent (as Socrates argued about 25 centuries ago). The hypnotic technique of *polar methods* is exemplified below.

Say, for example, we are approached by a client who complains of feeling a sort of heaviness that has tormented him for some time. We might suggest that he concentrates on (for instance) his two hands and identify the one in which the feeling he is complaining of is more pronounced. As we know, we are all capable of creating mental projections, so it would be easy for the client to discover this same feeling projected into one of his hands. After he has identified one hand as heavier, we might shift his attention to the other hand, on which we project the opposite feeling by means of suggestion – a sense of lightness and calm. We can thus help the client discover an alternative part of his self that he had forgotten even existed – yet sometimes all we need to learn to feel something again is to remember how it felt.

A therapeutic process always has turning points and critical situations. Similarly, in many cases the client's problem is that they are unconsciously deluding themselves that they are ill or that things stand in a particular way. Undoubtedly, in such cases one of the crucial moments is the instant in which clients reach a point where they can no longer delude themselves. If we succeed in reaching this point, our job from then on will be much more predictable and routine. For example, people suffering from hypochondria delude themselves that they have a disease or disorder. If we succeed in bringing them to a situation that will deprive them of any ability to cling on to such a delusion, we can get their maximum commitment to fulfilling various genuinely therapeutic tasks.

Here is another case that illustrates the issue in question.

This is a classic case of hypochondria. The client was Katya [not her real name], a woman of 43, who could not persuade herself that she did not suffer from every single disease she had ever heard of, despite the excellent and always positive results of the medical tests she was forever undergoing.

Even at our very first session I tried to introduce the idea that hers was a case of auto-suggestion – but I naturally failed because Katya could listen to nothing but her own fears. She was not really attending to anything I said and just kept on believing that she suffered from all the various diseases. What she was really suffering from was her self-delusion, whatever the causes of that might be.

Towards the end of the session I drew her attention to the importance of physical exercise. She agreed with me, and because she genuinely wanted to solve her problem, she accepted my suggestion of jogging every morning. Yet just before she left, she asked me a question that I was expecting because it was typical of her condition:

"Could jogging do me any harm?"

"Of course not," I replied. "But let's hope you won't get a pain in the back."

"Why?" she asked anxiously, "Should I?"

"Certainly not," I said. "Don't worry."

Of course, at the next session the first thing Katya told me was that she was doing what I had told her but definitely had a pain in her back. I told her that in all likelihood her body had not adapted to the strain yet, and that everything was all right considering that she had no pain in the knees.

"But should I have a pain in the knees?" she asked.

"Of course not," I replied. "Don't worry – and keep on jogging."

Then I changed the subject.

The next week Katya was rather anxious because she now had a pain not only in her back but also in her knees.

Pretending to be uneasy, I shook my head and told her:

"I don't believe we could have been wrong. Keep on jogging. If your heart's okay, there's nothing to worry about really."

"But could something go wrong with my heart?" Katya was now really worried.

"No," I said reassuringly, "there's no danger of that."

And I changed the subject again.

At the next session she turned up terrified and complained that along with the pain in her back and her knees, she now had a heart problem. Looking genuinely alarmed, I asked her if she had any problems with breathing.

"Why, yes," she said after a moment's self-inspection. "I can hardly breathe."

The situation was quite tense – which is a favourable context for therapeutic manipulation of the conscious mind. I decided to introduce a psychodramatic element. Pacing nervously up and down, I started blaming myself for the deterioration in her condition. I muttered to myself that I had no right to experiment on her, stared silently out of the window for several minutes and pretended that I did not notice her attempts to strike up a conversation. The situation became grotesque when half an hour later I was still fretting and fuming, oblivious to her presence and vain efforts to get through to me. We had switched our roles from our first session – now it was *she* who was trying to tell *me* something that I would not hear.

Finally Katya, who was entirely confused by then and eager to calm me down so as to refocus on her own problems, shook my elbow with the expression of someone explaining something self-evident to someone who is extremely stupid, and almost screamed in my face:

"Please stop worrying about it! *I'm only putting it on!*"

At that instant she froze. This was the turning-point in the therapeutic process. It was the first time that she had actually heard what everybody had been trying to tell her. Deluding herself was no longer an alternative. It is impossible to describe her shock at her own words.

I seized the opportunity to put her in a trance by entirely nonverbal means, and she told me about the shock she had suffered when she had seen a dead body for the first time at the funeral of a relative. It turned out that the fear of inevitable death was at the root of all her problems.

Her therapy subsequently changed tack. The purpose was to find the best way for Katya to channel in a positive direction the inevitable change that follows the loss of one's illusions.

After another two sessions, Katya decided to come off the tranquillisers that she had been living on for the previous three years. We arrived at the conclusion that she must take full responsibility for this decision, whatever the price. She said that she needed my help, since we had come to this point together and had to go on together. She saw my help as a period in which I had to be at her disposal as frequently as possible, or at least to increase our sessions from once to three times a week.

I refused, since that would maintain her illusion that she could not be independent. I even suggested that we end our sessions altogether. I told her that this was her chance to recover her self-confidence and to overcome her anxieties, because she could use the present moment of change to get better. If I were to be proved wrong, she would not benefit from continuing our sessions anyway. We arranged for her to call when and if she needed me.

Five weeks later Katya rang me up and told me how she had dropped the tranquillisers; she told me about the crisis that had caused, about her thoughts at the hardest times, and about the unsuspected *raison d'être* she had rediscovered in her life. She had the feeling that she was "born again".

We met once more and went over the entire therapeutic process and everything she had experienced. It was a discussion with someone who had lived through an incredibly difficult period in life that was now behind her, and who was ready to look ahead with interest, and not with fear.

That was Katya's case, the case of a person who simply needed to stop deluding herself that she was sick.

Next, I should say a few words about strategic tasks and therapeutic assignments – one of Erickson's favourite methods. The principle of this method is to link a task-

and-assignment to a specific symptom, the task itself being harder than the symptom. For example: a client complains that she is overweight and incapable of controlling her eating habits. An optimal diet by days and hours is drawn up with her approval. She may break the diet only if she completes an *assignment* – which she has also approved in advance – before and after. The assignment may be anything – e.g. a workout. So if she keeps to her diet, she does not need to do the physical assignment. On the other hand, every time she breaks the diet she must undergo a punishment which, in this particular case, in itself has a positive and curative effect.

A colleague of mine claims that this approach does not work because his patients refused to do any of the tasks he assigned them and their therapy therefore had no effect at all.

Let us note that the point here is not to invent an appropriate assignment – clients usually suggest that for themselves. The trick is to make them believe you and to commit themselves to doing their "homework". Yet for the purpose we must help motivate them to do sometimes difficult, unpleasant, or even bizarre things.

The parents of 16-year-old Petya [not her real name] brought her to see me because they thought she might have bulimia. Petya would vomit up most of her food. She sometimes threw up more than 15 times a day. She had started worrying about her health too, and wanted help.

Petya was an excellent hypnotic subject and easily entered deep trance. I guided her into hypnosis on a single occasion only, and the only thing I did then was to return her to third grade and make her write her name. Naturally, she used her handwriting as a third-grader, which is typical and normal in cases of age regression.

After I woke her, I showed her what she had written. She remembered nothing of what had occurred under hypnosis and was genuinely amazed. I took this opportunity to present the power of hypnosis to her virtually as a magic wand, while at the same time winning her confidence.

I explained that she would benefit from my therapy only if she performed various assignments at home, and she agreed.

The first week she had to record the exact time whenever she threw up, and she proved extremely meticulous in carrying out that "punishment".

The second week her assignment was to do a short set of physical exercises, which I had shown her, every time she threw up. This did not prove any problem for her either, and the number of times she threw up remained more or less the same.

As you may well be thinking, the only purpose of those otherwise meaningless assignments on my part was to get Petya used to carrying out the tasks I set her while checking her commitment to attaining improvement. I must say that I was pleasantly surprised by her determination to deal with her problem. The only thing she lacked was the knowledge of how to do it. In my attempts to help her find a favourable alternative, I decided to resort to the positive potential of her subconscious.

I had noticed at earlier sessions that Petya was very anxious about wasting my time. She thought that I had more serious things to do than deal with her. I did not try to persuade her that this was not true, because I realised that this gave me a strategically good opportunity for action.

And so, on the third week Petya's task was to ring me up every time she vomited, irrespective of the time and irrespective of whether I was at the office or at home. The only thing she had to tell me was "I've thrown up", and that was all. I also told her that if she did not carry out this task it would mean that all our work together so far had been a waste of time for both of us.

Her first call came shortly after our session that same day. She called again several hours later. The third call came at 1 a.m.

On the next day Petya called five times during the day-time and not at all during the night.

The day after she called twice. And she did not call again until the next session, when she apologised for having bothered me with her calls. Besides, she was surprised that she had not thrown up at all in the past five days, and boasted that she had put on two kilos.

We had another three sessions, the assignment remaining the same, but she didn't call once in the meantime. During those three sessions we discussed entirely different subjects and concerns.

Petya's subconscious had done its job and had taught her not to throw up – just as she had learned to throw up earlier.

At this point we might note that psychotherapy is very often a learning process. We can use learning in hypnotherapy too. We can teach our client how to relax, how to enter a trance, and how to apply different self-relaxation and other meditative techniques at times coinciding with their own chrono-biological rhythm, according to Ernest Rossi's theory mentioned earlier.

As noted before, hypnotherapy is a symptom-focused therapy designed to deal with a specific symptom as quickly as possible. Of course, we must always keep in mind the risk that this symptom might be replaced with another which also serves the previous need. Our purpose is therefore to change the client's overall view of things, his or her entire attitude to the world, to others and to the self – i.e. a change in his or her way of functioning at the cognitive and behavioural level.

In some cases our clients might know the particular event or situation that has caused their distress. In others we might search out the cause even when they have suppressed or forgotten it. Unlike analytical therapy, which works with interpretations rather than with things themselves, we can use hypnotherapy to help our clients reach the roots of their suffering. We can achieve this by following "the symptom path to enlightenment," as Ernest Rossi aptly called this technique. The logic here is remarkably simple: instead of assuming that a particular situation is the cause of a problem and endeavouring to repair the "mechanism" that is responsible for the outward signs of the problem (this is the principle of analytical therapy), we use the traumatic situation as our point of reference to reverse the direction and proceed from the present moment, in which the symptom manifests itself, and by means of regression trace it systematically back in time, thus – swimming against the tide – ultimately reaching the source. However, to follow the symptom path, the particular symptom should preferably be full-blown at the actual time of therapy.

Here is a sample case. The client complains of an indeterminate sense of fear and anxiety. The stronger he feels this symptom during the therapeutic session, the more favourable our conditions of work. We might put our client into a trance and suggest that he feels as acutely as possible the fear and anxiety that he has identified as a problem. When we are sure (through verbal or ideomotor communication with him) that this feeling has reached it climax, we might use a well-phrased suggestion to ask him to return to the moment (the situation) when he first felt exactly the same way.

In relation to this method, it must be said that we all have important events and unsolved things in our lives, and when we are under hypnosis it is precisely those important events and unsolved dilemmas that will take up our full attention. We know that this is possible and easy to achieve in trance, just as we know that a trance is the domain of freedom where everything is possible except lying.

We know perfectly well that hypnosis has been and is widely used in general medicine and in dentistry. In some cases its use is not only possible but practically unavoidable because there is no alternative – for example, when someone needs surgery urgently but is allergic to the available anaesthetics. In this case we cannot rely on anything but suggestion-induced anaesthesia. In fact, it is arguable that general medicine and dentistry *demand* the availability of the phenomenon that is hypnosis, which allows us to cope with pain as an invariable element in the practice of doctors and – especially – dentists.

Before proceeding to examine this question in detail, let us say briefly and clearly: yes, it is certainly possible to deal with physical pain with the help of hypnosis and suggestion only – and we do not normally need a deep hypnotic trance for the purpose. It is also possible to induce hypnosis in someone who is currently in immediate and urgent pain.

There are, then, several main hypnotic techniques to deal with pain. One of them involves another trance phenomenon – i.e. dissociation.

For example, if someone complains of pain in a recently-fractured arm, we might induce a sense of dissociation between this and the other arm or between this arm and the rest of the body. The logic is that if the broken arm does not belong to the body, the pain in it is also dissociated. This might sound absurd to some – and it *is* absurd, but only if we forget that we are talking about an altered state of consciousness such as hypnosis. In this context, we must remember that the most important thing remains genuine hypnotic communication.

We might achieve the same result with the help of polar methods – i.e. if one part of the body is warmer and the other is colder. In the same way, if one part of the body is more sensitive, the other might be perceived as more insensitive. In that example we might concentrate the client's attention on his or her healthy arm and maximise its sensitivity with the help of suggestion – in some cases this is enough to relieve the pain because the subconscious does the rest of the job. After all, there is no need to mention that there are windows in a room if we have already discussed the curtains.

Another orthodox variant is to induce numbness in a particular part of the body and to gradually spread anaesthesia to the whole body, including the sore or injured part.

Unfortunately, there is little to be said about what is probably the most effective way of dealing with pain – taking the pain or suffering outside the situational context itself. We all know about this method, and all we have to do is start exercising and applying it in practice. You cannot make people forget about a pain in their arm by telling them, "You no longer feel a pain in your arm." To take pain out of the context of the particular situation means to talk and do anything to distract, to burden the conscious mind in any way, to set any tasks, as long as they have nothing to do with pain or the arm that feels it. And the most important thing is that the client has not even the vaguest idea that the purpose of it all is to remove pain.

As a matter of fact, we can not only deal with a client's immediate and urgent pain but also use posthypnotic suggestion to lay the groundwork for our subsequent therapeutic work with that client. This could be applied successfully in dentistry, in obstetrics (many women today deliver their babies under hypnosis – i.e. awake, so that they remember this crucial event in their lives and help the midwife/doctor without being in any pain), in work with the terminally ill who are in constant pain (e.g. cancer patients) so that they can have a full life in their remaining time on earth, and in similar contexts. In general, there are plenty of occasions and scenarios in general medicine and dentistry in which hypnosis can be used. All we can do is hope that hypnotic methods will become increasingly popular among the various therapeutic communities.

Finally, I have decided to devote a few lines to my own truly modest contribution to the treasury of hypnotherapy. I would like to present a technique developed as a result of my hypnotic practice to date, and which for me has unequivocally proved its practical effectiveness. The technique is based on Coué's Law of reverse effort, according to which the harder a person tries to do something, the smaller is his or her chance of success. On the other hand, its theoretical justification rests on assumptions based on the overall characteristics and general functioning of our conscious and subconscious mind.

In addition to the techniques outlined above, then, there are also some that might look quite unrealistic at first glance. Nevertheless, their perfect simplicity (even though they can seem fairly complex) makes them extremely effective in practice. A truly effective hypnotic technique in dealing with physical pain, emotional distress or any other sensation, is the technique based on the principle of *paradoxical intention*. The best thing about this technique is that it cannot fail.

To explain it in detail, let us go back to the concrete example of pain in a recently-fractured arm. Our client complains that his arm hurts and that painkillers are ineffective. We know that pain has a signal function – i.e. we do not necessarily *have* to feel pain. This means that at the physical and mental level our body *has a choice* whether to feel pain or not to. In our role as hypnotists we might simply suggest to our client's subconscious how to make this choice. We must first keep in mind that our unconscious potential is incomparably larger than that of the conscious – which means that in a paradoxical situation that is incomprehensible for the conscious, the decisions are made by the unconscious part of our psyche.

And so, to return to the situation in question, we might take concrete action to deal with the problem. To use the paradoxical intention technique means to concentrate our client's conscious mind on the pain in his arm and to make him identify the exact boundaries of the aching spot. Next we ask him to try to increase the sensation of pain in that same spot as much as possible. We must keep in mind that trying to do something and actually doing it are two different things. This is important, because we are not instructing the conscious mind to actually increase the sensation of pain but only to *try* to do it. This is rather a strange situation – the person has turned to us to relieve his pain, yet we are asking him to increase it. In this case the conscious mind is entirely helpless to do anything (which is why the person has approached us – because he cannot cope with his problem in the normal state of consciousness). The final say therefore goes to the subconscious, which does not want to feel pain and has the resources to create anaesthesia.

This is also how this technique works – allowing the subconscious to deal with the problem by itself. No matter how hard the conscious mind strives to carry out its task – *trying* to increase the pain – it is doomed to fail in its sparring contest with the subconscious, which does not want to feel pain, and this contest is usually won by the subconscious by a knockout. In most cases the pain disappears – to the sincere astonishment of the client, who wonders how he can have failed to carry out his task.

However, the questions that you are probably asking

yourself right now are the obvious ones: *How can we possibly avoid all failures if the pain goes away in most cases only? What can be done in the other cases?* This is precisely where the power of this technique lies – if our client succeeds in increasing the sensation of pain, it means that he can also reduce it: we are thus giving him conscious *control* over the nature and extent of his sensations.

In brief, in applying the paradoxical intention technique, there are two possible alternatives.

The first and most common one is when our client is incapable of carrying out our requirement that he increase the intensity of his own suffering. In this case he practically resists us with the power of his subconscious, and the subconscious usually wins the battle in which, as noted earlier, we are on its side.

The second alternative is that our client really will succeed in carrying out our requirement, and so increase his own pain. This means, however, that he is also capable of reducing it. Or, in other words, in this event he is demonstrating a power of the conscious mind that enables him to manipulate the sensation that is negative for him.

Needless to say, this technique is applicable both in general medicine and in dentistry, but also in many cases of psychotherapy.

Here I would like to draw your attention to one peculiar aspect of psychotherapy. Unlike other exact sciences and activities, in psychotherapy we cannot rely on an objective and concrete assessment of the effectiveness of our work, or even on an ultimately final end-result. In fact, the only criterion for the efficacy of our actions remains our client's own feelings – subjective factors that have to be monitored over a sufficiently long period of time in order to be trusted. I know this sounds too simplistic and unreliable for some people, but this is how things stand when you are dealing with human beings. For it is extremely difficult to calculate the degree of increase and activation of your clients' positive potential, or, to put it simply, to judge how correct is the path they have chosen in their desire for a happy and full life.

Let me tell you something else too. There are also cases in which the therapist and the client disagree about the effectiveness of the therapy, but this does not necessarily mean that our approach was wrong. Let us remember that one of our main therapeutic goals must be to restore our clients' self-confidence in their own resources and potential. By the same logic, in most cases it is extremely beneficial to persuade them that in fact all progress made during the therapeutic process was entirely their own doing, thus making them believe in themselves rather than in us. If, however, we have done our job well, we must not expect too much gratitude from people we have helped; in that case they will have seen what what was there to be seen – their own power and potential, and not ours. We may say that we have been truly of help if we have led our clients to the point at which we have become useless and redundant to them – i.e. when they no longer need help from a therapist. But this must be a sufficient reward for those who understand and love psychotherapy as their profession.

At the same time, there are also quite a few cases in which the result of therapy is genuinely and indisputably final. It was so in the case of Ms Svetla Damyanova, whose name has not been changed because, for one thing,

I have obtained her full consent, and for another, I cannot resist telling her story – a story of well-deserved success which, at the same time, offers incontestable proof of the effectiveness of hypnosis when used properly.

Svetla had been actively involved in sports all her life, having passed through various disciplines in track and field, and winter sports and aerobics, to name but a few. She decided to become a professional weightlifter at the age of 32 and proved quite good at it, as a result of which she started training in the national weightlifting team. Three years later, she turned to me for help on the recommendation of someone we both knew. Her problem was that she believed her performance was far below her real potential. In fact, her results had not increased even by a single kilo in more than two years. In an effort to cope with this problem, Svetla had tried all sorts of things – including hypnotherapy, which, however, had proved ineffective. Nevertheless, she came to see me full of enviable optimism. She told me what her problem really was.

Briefly, Svetla competed in the 48 kg class, and her record was 60 kg snatch and 72.5 kg clean-and-jerk. At the same time, her scores should have been higher by at least 15 to 20 kg, since she was strong enough to squat with a 120 kg weight. That was the whole point.

I suggested to Svetla that we conduct an experiment so that I could get a clear idea of our prospects, and with her consent I hypnotised her (she proved to be an excellent hypnotic subject). I suggested directly that she mobilise all her resources and snatch 62.5 kg at the next practice session. She called me later that same day happy and enthusiastic, because she had improved her personal record for the first time in two years.

We proceeded to work seriously for several months, with Svetla consistently showing exceptional commitment, responsibility and discipline – qualities that an athlete cannot do without. The therapeutic process itself was highly dynamic, varied and interesting for both of us. I first had to learn from Svetla a lot of things about this difficult sport and design my strategy accordingly. On the other hand, the mental barriers that were preventing her from maximising her potential were revealed one by one. Almost 90 per cent of the therapy was conducted under hypnosis, three and occasionally four times a week. Direct suggestion played a minor role in this process, since the main purpose was to achieve a wider goal – namely, to improve the effectiveness of Svetla's functioning across the broadest possible range, covering different aspects of her mental and physical world. Still, we did have a specific goal, so we also worked on particular aspects of her training – physical strength, speed, technique, explosiveness, etc. At the same time, we also dealt actively with things such as motivation, positive thinking, confidence, and visualisation as part of training, concentration and control of attention, anxiety control, work under mental tension, etc. The result of all this was that Svetla achieved something few weightlifters can boast of – in just three months she improved her personal record by a combined total of almost 30 kg – i.e. to 75 kg snatch and 85 kg jerk, which placed her among the top ten weightlifters in the world. [I should make it utterly clear that Svetla never at any time before or during our work together used drugs or blood additives.]

But that is not all. From 8 to 14 October 2000, Orlando, Florida, hosted the 16th world weightlifting championships, involving 550 entrants from 41 countries. Svetla Damyanova represented Bulgaria. I was given the opportunity to attend the event in an official capacity as Svetla's personal coach. Naturally, my work was associated mainly with her mental training, as well as with the technicalities around her participation, because I had to act as a Bulgarian team-leader too. Unfortunately, two days before October 8, when she was scheduled to appear, Svetla injured her right knee – a nasty accident that not only horrified us (and indeed plunged us into despair) but also created an extremely tense situation that was ruinous to the emotional state an athlete needs in order to be in top shape. Nevertheless, we decided to take up the challenge.

The night before the competition I guided Svetla into hypnosis and did not wake her until the following day. While she was under hypnosis I literally "loaded" her with posthypnotic suggestions, aiming to deal both with her confidence and concentration during the competition as well as with the pain in her knee. The next morning she was faced with undoubtedly the greatest ordeal in her life, because it was now all down to her.

I won't keep you in suspense, so I will tell you right away that Svetla Damyanova needed only a single attempt in each event to win the gold medal by a margin of 17.5 kg ahead of the German runner-up. In the most adverse physical and psychological condition, Svetla became a world champion! I can hardly describe how moved I was while listening to the Bulgarian national anthem in a situation in which I had never imagined I would be in my whole life. Yet that is where the strange and attractive lore of hypnosis took me.

Needless to say, after those world championships many new doors for professional development opened up in front of Svetla, and that is actually the best way to gauge the effectiveness of our almost year-long collaboration. So there really are also cases in a psychotherapist's practice when the result is both obvious and final and saves us from questions about whether we are genuinely doing anything or if we only think that we are. I have to say that I am sure that those therapists who have never asked themselves questions like that are in a most unenviable position.

Only now, at this late stage, I remember that I have not finished the story I told you in Chapter 1 – about the martial arts student and his teacher.

And thus, after the teacher explained the necessary techniques in detail, he told his student the most important thing. He told him:

> The art of combat is learned in combat only. The hardest ordeal of a man is to face another man.

But all who work with people in one field or another know this. Others will learn it.

Chapter 10
Application: a few examples
of induction techniques

The process of putting a client under hypnosis has several stages: the preparation of the client for the trance, inducing the trance, deepening the trance, utilising the trance, and waking the client afterwards. Because of the flexible nature of the process it is difficult to describe it either in detail or in an apparent order. All the same, I feel that a few specific techniques and methods should be outlined. Our purpose is, after all, to turn our theoretical knowledge into practical skills. And in this area, as in any other, there are aspects of knowledge that can be systematised and act as background information on which further, more complex learning (perhaps under the guidance of an even better teacher) can then be based.

The next few pages are dedicated to that part of the hypnotic process that can be systematised in this way: I will describe some basic trance-induction techniques. Before you try them, however, you really ought to consider your responsibilities in relation to how effective as a hypnotist you think you will be. Don't start anything you can't stop. It may well be that you will decide that the best method is to approach the learning in the reverse order from the way you plan to use it – and start at the *end* of the hypnosis process. That is, you should start by first perfecting the "waking" script, since that will ensure your client's safety and security after the session. A second step will then be to learn off the "deepening" script, because it something that can be applied to every hypnotic induction. With the time and as you progress in competence, you may find that you can add to or alter elements in this process according to the specific factors of your cases. Only then, perhaps, should you attempt the induction techniques (which may also be added to or altered as necessary). In all things and at all times, however, remember that you are potentially changing people's lives – and in a way that must result in their benefit.

A standard waking script

When we awake our client from a trance, we speak faster, louder and more energetically than we do when we are inducing the trance. Otherwise, there is an incongruity between verbal and nonverbal expression that is not favourable. With a wrong approach, the client might feel discomfort in one form or another – something that should always be avoided.

The classic waking script goes something like this:

> In a while I am going to count from ten down to one
> ... On each count you will become more and more
> awake.
>> On each count your normal body tone will return
> in greater strength.
>> When I say "three", you will open your eyes,
> feeling refreshed and rested.
>> When I say "one", you will be completely awake
> and you'll be in a good mood. When I say "one" you
> will be back to normal here and now, in the same
> room, in the same chair, where we started the session
> ...
>> Ten, nine, eight, seven, six, five, four, three ...
> Open your eyes! ...
>> Two ...
>> One! Open your eyes and wake up! You're wide
> awake!

Towards the end of a session we may wonder whether the client has really been in a trance state at all. Even so, the session must nonetheless finish in this fashion – it is the only responsible thing to do!

A standard deepening script

At this stage your client is already sitting quietly with closed eyes following the induction into hypnosis you have already performed. You now speak in a slow and even voice.

> In a while I am going to count from one up to ten
> and at each count you will become more and more
> relaxed ... With each number your breathing will be-
> come slower ... deeper ... and more and more even
> ...

When I say "ten" … you will go into a deep and pleasant sleep … and nothing else will matter except my voice …

One …two …three … You don't have to do anything … You don't even have to try to go into a deep … deep … sleep with each number … becoming deeper and deeper every time you breathe in … and every time you breathe out …while you are listening to my voice… that helps you to get even more and more relaxed…

Four … and every desire to move disappears … and the slightest movement … the slightest trembling of your eyelids helps you to become sleepier and sleepier … more and more … while your breathing becomes deeper and calmer …

Five… six… and I wonder which part of you is in a deeper sleep – your body … or your mind …

Seven… and you can allow yourself to sink into this pleasant trance more and more … now! …

Eight …that's right! … Wonderful! …

Nine …

In a while you will hear me say "ten" … When in a while you hear me say "ten" … you will go into a deep and pleasant sleep … and nothing else will matter except my voice … And now you relax even more … and sleep!

Ten! Sleep! Go into a deep and calm sleep! That's right! Wonderful!

This is the right moment to apply some of the tests that show the depth of the trance state, so you will be able to decide what is best for you to do next.

Now, trusting that you have paid proper attention to everything described up to this point, I append some of the most popular and effective trance-inducing techniques.

Induction using two fingers on one hand

Get your subject to sit in a chair as you stand in front of him or her. You then begin speaking in a calm and slow voice.

> And now just relax and make yourself comfortable. Rest your arm upon your knees. Now I want you to follow my right hand with your eyes while you're relaxing more and more ... Now I want you to look here at my hand. In a moment I'm going to bring my hand up in front of your eyes like this ...

(Meanwhile you place your hand with the index and the middle finger outstretched in the form of letter V somewhere in front of the subject's eyes at the level of his or her eyebrows.)

> ... I want you to move your eyes to follow the tips of my fingers without moving your head ... You may feel that your eyes are getting tired while your breathing is getting deeper and calmer ...

(You hold your hand for a while at eyebrow level to cause tiredness in the subject's eyes and then you start lowering your hand in front of his or her face, your two outstretched fingers pointing directly at each of his or her eyes. You continue with the verbal suggestions.)

> ... I want you to try not to close your eyes yet ... although you will feel your eyelids getting heavier and heavier ...

(You continue slowly lowering your fingers.)

> … They are getting heavier and heavier … with every breath you take … with every word I say … As your eyelids become as heavy as lead … you can feel the muscles of your eyes becoming more and more tired … That's right! … I know that it is difficult for you to try to keep your eyes open … while you're following the fingers of my hand … but in a while you can allow yourself to close them and to get into a deep and pleasant sleep … Now! … That's right!

(When your fingers reach the bottom of the subject's level of sight, his or her eyes are almost closed – and this is the moment to continue in an authoritative voice.)

> Close your eyes! Close your eyes! … That's right! … Close them and relax … Sleep! … And as you're falling even deeper and deeper asleep … you may notice how relaxed the muscles of your eyes are … So pleasantly relaxed … and it's difficult for you to open them even if you try, because every desire to move has melted away … I know that this will make you even more tired, but you can try to open your eyelids, which are very … very … heavy …

(Closely observing the subject's attempts or inability to open the eyes, you will have a better idea of how to continue with the session.)

> And now you just relax … That's right! … Wonderful!

If you are happy with the result, you can now go on to apply a deepening technique.

The form of induction described above is of the authoritarian type and actively invokes the physical tiredness of the eyes.

Induction by dropping a coin

This is a very popular technique. Again get your subject to sit in a chair. One of his or her arms is stretched straight out in front and between the thumb and index finger of that hand he or she holds a coin. You begin speaking.

> Now close your eyes and think of that coin between the thumb and index finger of your right hand ... I want you to look at it ... I wonder if you will notice the moment when it will become very heavy and it will be difficult for you to keep holding it ... and when you hear the sound of the coin dropping on the floor, you will close your eyes and you will go into a deep and pleasant sleep ...
>
> You can feel the coin getting heavier and heavier between your fingers as your breathing gets deeper and slower ... as you become more and more relaxed ... That's right! ...
>
> You can feel your arm getting heavier and heavier with every breath you take ... with every word I say ... And as you are listening to my voice ... and relaxing even more ... the coin is getting heavier and heavier ...
>
> And the slightest movement ... the slightest trembling of your arm makes you more and more sleepy ... and more and more drowsy ... I see how difficult is for you to hold the coin between your fingers ... and how ... the heavier your arm becomes, the heavier your eyelids become too ... and your breathing is slow and deep ... very deep ...
>
> That's right! ... Don't take your eyes from the coin...

(Usually the subject very soon drops the coin and at that moment we give the following instructions in a firm voice.)

> Close your eyes! Now! Close your eyes and sleep! ...
> Sleep! ... Go into a deep and calm sleep ...

It is possible for some subjects to go to sleep with the arm still stretched out, in which case we can give them an instruction to lower it and to make themselves comfortable for the rest of the session. Then we can go on with a trance-deepening technique if required.

The strong point of this form of induction is the fact that it distracts the attention of the subject from the suggestions we are giving and makes him or her concentrate on the coin. Usually people put all their effort into not dropping it or at least holding it for as long as possible. All their negative energy thus focuses on the coin and not on our relaxing suggestions, which therefore reach the subject's subconsciousness totally unhindered. In other words, the longer the subject holds the coin, the better for the hypnotic process, because we have enough time to implant all the suggestions we need to.

Induction by eye-closing

Get the subject to sit in a chair and ask him or her to close the eyes. You begin speaking.

> I'm going to count from five down to one. As I do, your eyelids will lock tightly closed so that the more you try to open them, the tighter they stay locked and closed.

Five ... Your eyes are pressing down tightly ...

Four ... pressing down and sealing shut ...

Three ... sealing as if they were glued together ...

Two ... They're locked shut. The more you try to open them, the tighter they're staying locked and closed.

Okay – try to open your eyelids now and find them locking tighter and tighter. That's fine. You can stop trying now. Just relax and go into deeper sleep.

You then continue (if appropriate) with the deepening script.

Induction by nonverbal handshake

As we said above, we can imply a suggestion in a nonverbal way too. This induction is a good example of this. We start by getting the subject to sit in a chair, facing us. We hold his or her hand and we start slowly and evenly, following the subject's breathing pattern, to lower and raise the two clasped hands as if being introduced. We look at the subject's eyes all the time. Every time he or she blinks, we hold the hands down for a few seconds, after which we resume the previous motions. Little by little we endeavour to slow down the rhythm. In this way we subconsciously associate the movement of the hand and the closing of the eyes, which implants the nonverbal suggestion of sinking into sleep. Trance indicators will become apparent to us after a while, and when the subject eventually closes his or her eyes for a little longer, we can further enhance the rapport by saying in a calm and confident voice:

> That's right! Wonderful! You sleep now! Sleep! The only thing that you will be able to hear in your pleasant and deep sleep will be my voice! And now, just sleep!

We can go on at this stage to use the deepening script if required.

An example of rapid induction

Get the subject to sit in a chair. Maintain constant eye-contact and begin speaking:

> Are you ready to go into a deep and tranquil sleep?

After his or her confirmation, continue:

> In a while I am going to count from one up to three and I want you to take a deep breath with each number you hear me say. Every time you breathe out you will feel the muscles of your eyes and your face getting more and more relaxed. When you hear me say "three", your eyes will close and you will go into a deep and pleasant sleep ...
> And now ... One...
> Take a deep breath in and as you breathe out again I want you to feel the muscles of your eyes relaxing more and more ...You can feel a pleasant warmth spreading through your entire body ...That's right!
> Two ... Take another deep breath and feel a pleasant tiredness in your eyes ... They are so relaxed that you can allow them to start slowly closing as you're going into a deep and calm sleep ... and nothing else matters but my voice ...

Three ... Close your eyes! That's right! ...
You're more and more relaxed and more and more
drowsy ... All your muscles are relaxed and even
though your desire to move has disappeared I want
you to try to open your eyes, no matter how difficult it is ... After that you can close them again and
you'll relax even more, and you'll go into a deep
and pleasant sleep ...

(At the precise moment the subject tries to open his or
her eyes we just say in a firm voice:)

You can't open them! You know you can't! And
now just relax again and go to sleep! That's right!
Sleep!

The trick here is to discourage the subject from trying to open the eyes before he or she has even started. We
have to make the subject believe that he or she has failed
before even trying!

All these techniques work. They have a place among the instruments of most hypnotists. They are just examples drawn
from the huge repertoire of hypnotic inductions and they are
easy to use. But again – they are easy to use only after we
have spent an appropriate amount of time on all the other
things described in this book.

Conclusion

Dear reader! I want to share an observation that I made while I was writing this book ... which I am hoping you will have read. I noted down a couple of what I have to say are fairly obvious analogies between human life and books.

First, both have a beginning and an end, and they have their own history.

In addition, both contain good parts and not-so-good parts.

However, I believe that the most important thing is that every life and every book has its own mission, its own destination, which it may or may not successfully reach.

I wrote that last sentence because I am sure that this book has omitted a great deal that could have been usefully included.

But if somebody – it might be you – would like to make up those omissions and shed light on the areas that I have left so far unilluminated, then this book will have accomplished its mission.

I wish you every success!

References

Bandler, Richard (November 1989) *The Structure of Magic: A book about language and therapy.* Palo Alto, CA, USA. Science and Behavior Books

Bandler Richard and Grinder John (Vol.1, 1975; Vol.2, 1976) *Patterns of the Hypnotic Techniques of Milton H. Erickson, M.D.* Cupertino/Capitola, CA, USA, Calif. Meta Publications

Bandler, Richard and Grinder, John (1981) *Frogs Into Princes: Neuro-Linguistic Programming.* Moab, Utah, USA. Real People Press

Braid, James (1843) *Neurypnology, or The Rationale of Nervous Sleep, Considered in Relation with Animal Magnetism.* London, UK.

Bull, Stephen J., Albinson John G. and Shambrook Christopher J. (1996) *The Mental Game Plan: Getting psyched for sport.* Leicestershire, UK. Sports Dynamics

Castaneda, Carlos (1968) *The Teachings of Don Juan: A Yaqui Way of Knowledge.* Berkeley, CA, USA. University of California Press

Castaneda, Carlos (1972) *Journey to Ixtlan.* Berkeley, CA, USA. University of California Press

Castaneda, Carlos (1974) *Tales of Power.* Berkeley, CA, USA. University of California Press

Christenson, Allen J. (translator) (2003) *Popol Vuh: The sacred book of the Mayas.* **Oakland, CA, USA.** O Books

Erickson, Milton H. (February 1977) *Hypnotic Realities: The induction of clinical hypnosis and forms of indirect suggestion.* Hoboken, NJ, USA. John Wiley & Sons Inc.

Erickson, Milton H. with Rossi, Ernest L. (1989) *The February Man: Evolving consciousness and identity in hypnotherapy.* New York, NY, USA. Brunner-Mazel Inc.

Frankl, Viktor E. (2004) *Man's Search For Meaning.* London, UK. Rider

Freud, Sigmund (1991) *The Interpretation of Dreams*. London, UK. Penguin Books

Freud, Sigmund (1990) 'The Ego and the Id', in *The Complete Psychological Works of Sigmund Freud* (translation edited by James Strachey). New York, NY, USA. W W Norton & Co.

Gilligan, Stephen G. (1986) *Therapeutic Trances: The cooperation principle in Ericksonian Hypnotherapy*. New York, NY, USA. Brunner-Mazel Inc.

Grinder, John (1989) *The Structure of Magic* (Book 2): *A book about communication and change*. Palo Alto, CA, USA. Science and Behavior Books

Haley, Jay (1993) *Uncommon Therapy: The psychiatric techniques of Milton H. Erickson, M.D.* New York, NY, USA. W W Norton & Co.

Hammond, D. Corydon (1990) *Handbook of Hypnotic Suggestions and Metaphors*. New York, NY, USA. W W Norton & Co

Havens, Ronald A. (2004) *The Wisdom of Milton H. Erickson: Human behavior and psychotherapy*. Carmarthen, UK. Crown House Publishing

Heller, Steven and Terry Sheele (1988) *Monsters and Magical Sticks, or There's No Such Thing As Hypnosis*. Petaling Jaya, Malaysia. New Falcon Publications

Herrigel, Eugen (1953; trans. 1981) *Zen in the Art of Archery*. New York, NY, USA. Pantheon Books/Random House

Huxley, Aldous (1954/1956; 2004) *The Doors of Perception*, and *Heaven and Hell*. London, UK. HarperCollins

King, Mark E. and Citrenbaum, Charles M. (1994) *Existential Hypnotherapy*. New York, NY, USA. Guilford Press

Lao Tzu (2003) *Tao Te Ching* (translator Jonathan Star). New York, NY, USA. Jeremy P. Tarcher

Lloyd, David and Rossi, Ernest L. (1992) *Ultradian Rhythms in Life Processes: An inquiry into fundamental principles of chronobiol-

ogy and psychobiology. Berlin, Germany. Springer-Verlag Berlin and Heidelberg GmbH

Meadows, Kenneth (2001*) The Medicine Way.* London, UK. Rider

Moreno, Jacob L. (1977) *Who Shall Survive? Foundations of sociometry, group psychotherapy and sociodrama.* Boston, MA, USA. Beacon House

Musashi, Miyamoto (2004) *The Book of Five Rings.* London, UK. Allison & Busby

Nietzsche, Friedrich (2003) *Thus Spake Zarathustra* (translation by Thomas Wayne). New Delhi, India. Algora Publishing

NLP Comprehensive (1996) *NLP: The New Technology.* Norwood, MA, USA. Nicholas Brealey Publishing

Overdurf, John and Silverthorn, Julie (1995) *Training Trances: Multi-level communication in therapy and training.* Portland, OR, USA. Tad James/Metamorphous Press

Pirsig, Robert M. (1974) *Zen and the Art of Motorcycle Maintenance: An inquiry into values.* New York, NY, USA. William Morrow

Pirsig, Robert M. (1992) *Lila: An inquiry into morals.* London, UK. Bantam

Plato (1997) *Complete Works.* Indianapolis, Indiana, USA. Hackett

Rosen, Sidney (ed.) (1991) *My Voice Will Go With You: The teaching tales of Milton H. Erickson, M.D.* New York, NY, USA. W W Norton & Co.

Sun Tzu (2003) *The Art of War.* Philadelphia, PA, USA. Running Press

Watts, Alan W. (1957; 1989) *The Way of Zen.* New York, NY, USA. Vintage/Random House

Yogananda, P. (1996) *Autobiography of a Yogi.* London, UK. Rider